One
Breath
at a
Time

One Breath at a Time

at a

Lessons on Grief and Growth

GABRIELLE SHIOZAWA

DESERET
BOOK

All photos courtesy of the author. Photo on page 161 taken by Rey of Light Photography.

© 2021 Gabrielle Shiozawa

All rights reserved. No part of this book may be reproduced in any form or by any means without permission in writing from the publisher, Deseret Book Company, at permissions@deseretbook.com. This work is not an official publication of The Church of Jesus Christ of Latter-day Saints. The views expressed herein are the responsibility of the author and do not necessarily represent the position of the Church or of Deseret Book Company.

DESERET BOOK is a registered trademark of Deseret Book Company.

Visit us at deseretbook.com

Library of Congress Cataloging-in-Publication Data
(CIP on file)
ISBN 978-1-62972-915-2

Printed in the United States of America
PubLitho, Draper, UT

10 9 8 7 6 5 4 3 2 1

To Dad

Dear Reader,

We don't talk enough about how to grapple with the messy side of grief. It is a subject we brush under the rug because it makes us uncomfortable. Our ball-and-chain. The elephant in the room. Grief is isolating, devastating, and unfathomably heavy.

I was not ready to meet grief when it barged into my life unexpectedly at age eighteen, three weeks before I was to graduate from high school. I had no idea how many questions I'd have. How angry I would feel at everyone and no one, how PTSD would cloud my vision and alter my personality, how my entire way of life would change overnight.

This is the book I wish I'd had when my whole world came crashing down.

This is the book I wrote while I was picking up all those pieces and asking God how to make sense of them.

This is the book that helped me heal. I hope it will help you heal, too.

Maybe you don't know how to make sense of your new range of emotions. Maybe your life suddenly seems too heavy to bear, you're wondering how a loving God would let this happen, or you can't figure out how to keep moving forward. Perhaps you haven't lost anyone yet but want to have greater empathy for a grieving friend. Maybe other trials and life circumstances are causing you to feel broken. Irreparable. Alone.

We all have different stories, and I have been unusually blessed to have so many friends and supporters at my side while I have grieved. No matter your circumstances, I hope you will feel a sense of solidarity and find connections in these pages. Whether you walked through the valley hand in hand with loved ones or you are now trekking through it on your own, I hope you know that we are in this together. I hope that my authenticity and my weaknesses will help you find strength.

This book tells the story of my grief and my growth through the eyes of an earnestly awkward teenager trying to figure things out. It is a love letter to my father, Troy Kent Shiozawa. It is a story of hope. Most of all, this book is the story of the healing power of the Atonement of Jesus Christ. It is the story of how Christ took the darkest moments of my life and helped me turn them into something beautiful.

I know He will do the same for you.

Love,

Gabrielle

Fields That Were Not His Own

There are events in all of our lives that we anticipate resentfully rather than willingly. We grit our teeth as we set out to pull weeds, attend a sibling's barely rehearsed recital, or watch a poorly reviewed movie. We decide from the start that we are only going to push through to the finish line instead of enjoying the journey. Although I have worked on improving my outlook, there are still moments that find me grumbling and searching for brighter times ahead instead of enjoying the ones I'm in. I forget, in short, that there is good in everything.

It was September 2018, and for the first time in several years, my family was embarking on the awful eight-hour drive to Pocatello, Idaho, to visit my father's family. The main source of my dread was the long journey, but the anticipation of spending time with ill-acquainted relatives left me feeling apprehensive as well. My plan was to fill as much of the time as possible with a stack of mystery novels I'd picked up from the library.

I was uninterrupted in my reading for most of the car ride. That is, until we crossed the Utah-Idaho border and entered my dad's home state.

"Look!" my dad shouted as we passed a sign that read, "Welcome to Idaho!"

I nodded quickly in response, eager to get back to *The Curious Incident of the Dog in the Night-Time*, but my dad wasn't done talking. He pointed out a creek and a nearby cluster of homes. Gesturing to the fishermen we saw camping along the shore, Dad told me that my late great-grandfather, George Shiozawa, had often gone fishing along that same shoreline in his youth.

The closer we got to my dad's hometown of Pocatello, the more stories Dad had to tell.

"There's the hill where I ran cross-country!" he enthused as he pointed out a section of land that, once barren, was now covered with buildings and roads. "We ran all the way up that mountain, too. You see that path there, between the two poles? That's where we went."

He pointed out a field he farmed . . . and another . . . and another.

"That's the house where my first-grade teacher lived," he said. "Oh, and here's where my best friend used to live!"

I finally put my bookmark in and slammed the book closed, exasperated. I was seventeen and irritable. My legs were cramped and my little brothers were shrieking. Reading, my only form of escape, was being interrupted by a history lesson I hadn't asked for.

When we arrived at my grandparents' home in Pocatello, we gave hugs and kisses and settled in for a long weekend of cooking, eating, and enjoying time together.

The next day, we piled back into the truck, this time tailed by a carful of cousins, and traveled to nearby Blackfoot for the Idaho State Fair.

I thought the brief trip would be the perfect time for me

to return to my book, but my dad had other plans. He pointed out building after building, field after field, giving me a visual history of his youth as we traveled along the I-15. I grumbled and debated taking notes, as if the details of these stories might be later found on a pop quiz.

"You see that building there?" Dad asked, gesturing to a white-brick convenience store to our left. "I can't believe that store is still there; that's the wall I crashed into, right there."

I looked up in surprise, my curiosity piqued.

Huh, I smiled. *My dad wasn't always the perfect driver I thought he was.*

Farther along, my father pointed out a wide dirt road, a dilapidated barn, and a silver pickup truck.

"The house I grew up in was there by that barn, about where that truck is," Dad said.

"Why isn't the house there anymore?" I asked.

"It was just really old," my dad replied with a shrug. "It was a crappy old house. Someone else bought the property and decided to tear it down, I guess."

He was stalwart, unfazed, about this major part of his history that was now gone. As I mulled over his story, I pictured the only boyhood snapshot I could remember seeing of him. He was five years old, wearing a bright red shirt and an oversized cowboy hat, sitting on the back of a brown pony. I pictured that same little boy on that deserted farm in the middle of nowhere.

My heart was finally beginning to soften as I processed my father's anecdotes. I thought I knew a lot about the man who raised me, but every story he told managed to surprise me.

We were miles and miles down the highway when my father pointed out a series of long, green fields.

"I used to farm these fields when we lived in that house back there," he told me. "I would get on my horse and ride all the way down here, and the farmers would pay me to plant in these fields."

I pictured the tiny boy from the photograph riding all this way to labor, to plant, and to harvest in these fields that were not his own.

The thoughts that ran through my mind the next day, more than any memories of delicious fried foods or fast roller coasters at the state fair, were of my father's childhood stories. I was mulling over his comments about the house he grew up in when my grandma entered the living room with a stack of boxes in her arms. All the relatives were sprawled across

Dad, age 2, and his pony, Sally, in May 1972.

couches and rugs, dozing, but we sat up when we saw what was inside the containers.

Photographs. Stacks and stacks of photographs.

We gathered around her, intrigued. My dad traveled back in time to his youth, yet again, as he pored over yellowed photographs and crumbling newspaper clippings I had never seen before. We giggled as we passed the pictures around, amused by the bowl cuts, Coke-bottle glasses, and once-trendy fashion items that my father and his siblings had donned growing up in the seventies and eighties. We examined fuzzy exposures of generations of Shiozawas, drinking in a part of my father's history that, before obscured, was now in vivid color.

Now, as I look back on a weekend—and a life—that I have learned to enjoy and not just endure, I see snapshot after snapshot of my father's past through new eyes. I see the little Japanese boy with the messy hair, the boy who grew up hardworking and poor and still found reasons to smile every day.

I see Troy Shiozawa, the boy who grew up and became my father, the boy who's provided for his family and made sure that we never go without. My father has instilled in his children the same values of hard work and perseverance that he gained as a child growing up in southeastern Idaho, but he has done so without making us go through any of the trials that he did.

My dad saw the bright sunshine that comes from a life that is lived in service. My dad saw the good in everything.

May Day

I grew up in Moapa Valley, a small and close-knit community in Southern Nevada, where it is a valley-wide tradition to attend the May Day dances each year. Put on by Bowler Elementary the first Friday of each May, this century-old practice involves colorful homemade costumes, community raffles, and elementary-aged children dancing in everything from square dances to discos. Maybe it's because of the cheesy moves or the length of the event, but people who didn't grow up performing in May Day seem to avoid it when possible or attend begrudgingly.

Such was the case with my parents. My mom had grown up in Western Washington, and she and my Idahoan dad groaned as they dragged our family to yet another May Day dance. My brother Kenji was to perform in the second graders' Mexican hat dance, and he was dressed to the nines in neatly ironed clothes and shiny black shoes.

It was Friday, May 3, 2019.

Despite my parents' initial reservations, this was the best May Day I can remember. The acts flew by in a flurry of color. Kenji, despite being as mortified as every other eight-year-old boy at the prospect of having to dance with a girl, performed wonderfully. And then it was over. The last notes of the Bee

Gees' "Staying Alive" were fading as the sun began to set, casting long shadows across the fairgrounds. The cloud of dust billowing in the parking lot from the day's commotion gradually dispersed, leaving it empty and quiet.

We were among the stragglers, in no rush to leave the evening behind. We stayed for around an hour after the show, catching up with friends. Kenji had already made his way to a friend's birthday party, so it was just the four of us—Mom, Dad, two-year-old Sam, and me.

Our friend Brian teased my dad about the sugar skull on his T-shirt.

"It's Cinco de Mayo on Sunday!" Dad explained with a grin. "I can't wear this then because I'll be in a suit and tie. So I'm wearing it today!"

"Why don't you have a Mexican tie, Troy?" Brian asked, amused.

"I don't know," Dad said, giving me a pointed look. "But my birthday and Father's Day are both coming up."

"I'll get on it," I grinned. Picking out special gifts for my dad was my favorite challenge. It involved year-round note-taking and paying special attention to everything he got excited about. Dad always wanted to have a cactus in place of a Christmas tree, so I searched until I found the perfect fake cactus and covered it with tiny LED lights. (He said he put it in his closet and turned on the lights every morning while he was getting dressed for the day because it made him so happy.) When he showed repeated excitement over the almond cookies in *Kung Fu Panda*, I baked him an enormous stash. That night at the May Day dances, even as the conversation began moving in other directions, I began adding to my mental list of all the fun things I wanted to do for my dad for the holidays ahead.

My dad is so easy to love.

It was getting late when at last we waved goodbye to our friends and meandered back across the grass to our car. Suddenly, an idea seized me.

"You know, it's really nice out tonight," I said to Dad. "Maybe we should go on a run."

"Yes! Perfect," Mom latched onto the idea. "You should go running together right when we get home."

Every summer when we visited my mom's hometown, she and I competed in their Fourth of July footrace. Inspired by the 2018 event, Dad suggested he start training to race with us the next time around. That was ten months ago. My dad had not put on a pair of running shoes in that whole time.

Dad grabbed baby Sam's hand and slowly jogged across the grass with him.

"I'm already jogging," he said. "That's enough running for me tonight."

I looked back at Dad and Sam, hand in hand, and had a strong prompting come to my mind: *Take a picture.*

No, I thought. *I take too many pictures. I don't need to document everything.*

The thought came again to take out my phone and take a picture.

No, I replied stubbornly. *It's in my camera bag; I'd have to fish it out. It's cute, but I don't need to take a picture of it.*

That's the image that is burned in my brain: my dad and my baby brother running together. Dad, in that silly sugar skull shirt and his starched blue jeans. Dad, illuminated in the last golden rays of sun. I want to hold that imaginary photo in my hand and never let it go. Dad's childlike smile. Sam's short legs trotting to keep up. How they were both laughing.

I wish so desperately that I had taken that picture. I wish that I had followed that crystal-clear prompting that I so stubbornly cast aside.

It haunts me.

The Last First Run

Dad complained in a constant stream as we drove home, yet he was ready to go running before I was. I turned around and there he was in his black sugar skull shirt, black basketball shorts, and white sneakers, waiting for me.

I ran upstairs to change into workout clothes, slipping on the pink-and-gray sneakers Dad had bought me for cross-country at the beginning of the school year. Once I was ready, Dad and I headed to the corner of our driveway and began jogging north up Palo Verde.

Dad had me busting up laughing from the beginning.

"I don't WANNA!" he exclaimed, scrunching up his face and shaking his head dramatically from side to side. He fake-cried as he jogged along beside me. "Don't make me! I don't WANNA!"

"I don't know what you're complaining about!" I gasped between fits of laughter. "You're already doing better than I am!"

He was going faster than I had planned on taking him, his arms swinging perfectly at his sides, his stride consistent. I was impressed. He could joke all he wanted; for all the years that had passed since he'd last laced up his sneakers, he was still a powerful runner.

ONE BREATH AT A TIME

He pointed to our neighbor's circular driveway as we passed it on our left.

"Ah, look!" he said. "A lovely little detour. Let's just . . . take that and turn around and go home."

"Dad!" I laughed. "No, come on! Let's keep going!"

The sound of rushing water in a ditch grew louder as we neared the end of the street.

"Ah, behold: the beautiful babbling of the brook," Dad joked, gesturing with flourish. "Let's just take a nice rest here and then turn around."

"Dad! Stop!" I was laughing so hard my stomach ached.

Dad joked and complained and made me double over laughing all the way to the end of Palo Verde. As we turned left onto Willow, however, he stopped abruptly on the dusty road.

"Sorry," he said with a gulp. "I need to walk for a minute."

"No worries," I said. "You're doing great; we can walk."

We were quiet for a few minutes, running and walking intermittently along the dusty path. By the time we made it to the end of the road, my watch said we had only gone 0.65 miles.

"That was a lot," said Dad. "I think I need to turn around."

He was breathing hard, but he was still moving fast. My dad, invincible, the powerhouse. We turned around and started running back.

It wasn't long before he needed to stop again. He let out a loud burp.

"Gross, Dad!" I laughed, waving my hand in front of my face. A few steps later he burped again.

"Ugh," he said, shaking his head forcefully and swallowing hard.

Indigestion. Heartburn. There are other signs, too, that he probably felt but did not name. I don't know if he thought this was simply the struggle of getting back into shape or if he recognized their severity and simply didn't want me to know.

Pain and fatigue. Lightheadedness and sweating. Dizziness and discomfort. These are signs of hard exercise, especially for one who hasn't run in a long, long time.

But they are also signs of heart failure.

⨯⨯

We picked up our feet again. We stopped to walk just twice more, and then we were back on the road we'd started on, heading south towards the lights of home.

Dad started griping again as we passed the roaring waters of our neighbor's ditch, and I giggled.

"We just have to make it to the door, we're so close," I encouraged.

"Oh, I'm not making it to the door. I'm stopping here," Dad joked as he stepped onto our driveway. He bent over, breathing hard, and I put my hand on his back.

"You did really well," I beamed. "Come on. Let's go in."

We walked to the door, and he rolled onto the carpet in the entryway. Lying on his back, he gasped for air and joked about how mean I'd been by making him go for a run.

"You're not supposed to lie down right after you run!" I told him.

He climbed to his feet then bent over again, supporting himself with the arm of the couch.

"Oh," he whispered, clutching his chest. "I need oxygen. I need help."

I frowned and went to put my arm around him. I wasn't worried about him—I knew he was invincible—but I did want to help him if he needed it. I encouraged him to lean his weight on me so I could help him stand.

He turned his head just slightly so that his twinkling eyes could meet my own. Teasing, he whispered, "I'm kidding, Boo. I'm fine."

I felt silly, then, for having taken him seriously. He was always joking like that. Of course he was fine.

"You really did a good job," I said, straightening up. "Once school gets out, we can start getting up early and go running before you go to work."

"Right," Mom teased as she joined us from the kitchen. "Because the only thing Dad loves more than running is getting up early."

I smiled, shook my head, and patted Dad on the back.

"I'm heading out for another run," I said. "We didn't go very far."

"Yes, go ahead," he said, straightening up and waving me out the door. He grimaced. "I kept you from going longer! I'm sorry."

"No worries!" I said, touching his arm as he leaned on the couch again. "Seriously, you did great, Dad. That was really fun."

As I closed the front door behind me and headed back out into the fading twilight, I began imagining everything to come. Mom, Dad, Sam, and I would drive down to Maverik that night to get sodas, and then we'd come back and find something to watch together while we snuggled up on the couch. Kenji would come home from his party and join us. There was still pepperoni pizza from Costco on the counter. It was a perfect night.

I daydreamed about the weeks to come, too. I couldn't wait to take my dad running again. Every morning. All season long. I could see it before my eyes—an entire glorious summer of training together, racing together.

I was already picturing the victory of the finish line.

I had a million other adventures planned for the two of us as well. Skydiving and giant roller coasters. Baseball games and delicious foods. An endless list of things we loved that we could experience together, satisfying our tastebuds and giving us the adrenaline rush we craved.

Dad, Kenji, Sam, Po the Panda, and me at Universal Studios in Orlando, November 2018.

I was about to graduate high school, and then who knew where we could go or what we could do together? The possibilities were endless.

This run was supposed to be only the beginning.

They're Always Headed Somewhere Else

I set out at a sprint towards the paved half of the neighborhood. My mind was calm. I breathed in the faded gray sky, the tiny sparkling stars just beginning to emerge. Behind the mesas to the west, the ashy orange lights of Vegas were beginning to glow.

I'd only gone half a mile when I felt a prompting that I was supposed to go home. I didn't recognize it as such at the time; I reasoned to myself that it was late, that I was tired, that I was ready to go home to be with my family.

But before I turned around, I stood there in the middle of the road for a moment. I tilted my head all the way back and gazed upward, breathless from running and from pure delight, drinking in the faintly sparkling stars all above and around me. Then I jogged back home.

I was in the driveway, the outlines of orange lights above the garage casting shadows on the concrete in front of me, when I had the thought to go check the trampoline in the backyard. It was about 8:30 p.m. I'd been planning a stargazing party with some friends for around the same time the following evening, and I wanted to make sure the summer stars would cooperate with my plans.

As I lay there on the trampoline, still catching my breath,

there was a strange mix in my stomach of peacefulness and foreboding, a combination of feelings I couldn't place. I was only faintly aware of the sirens blaring in the distance, steadily growing louder.

Sirens, I mused faintly. *They're always headed somewhere else.*

Satisfied with the brightness of the stars, I jumped down from the trampoline and marched up the concrete steps to our back door. I knew it would be locked, but I also knew I could knock and have my family let me in instead of having to walk all the way around to the front.

But my family wasn't in the living room turning on the television, nor were they laughing and teasing each other in the kitchen. My dad was not chasing my little brother on all fours, growling, while Sam shrieked and laughed.

Instead, what I saw through the glass door was my mom's blonde ponytail bobbing up and down behind the couch. Her frantic movements. Sam running back and forth, babbling innocently, inaudibly.

And my dad.

All I could see of my dad were his pale legs sticking out from behind the couch.

Motionless.

His white sneakers. His black running shorts. He was there, on the carpet.

And suddenly the sirens were coming to my house, growing louder and louder, and in that moment, even though I couldn't process it and refused to believe it, I knew exactly why they were on their way.

ONE BREATH AT A TIME

This isn't real, I thought. *This kind of thing doesn't happen. This is a bad dream.*

No, I corrected myself. *This is the* worst *dream.*

I walked in a trance towards the sirens, towards the east edge of the porch. I saw bright red lights glowing through the pine trees, moving west towards the front of my house.

On the outside, I was calm and quiet.

But I was no longer in my body. The legs that wobbled and stumbled and finally dashed back onto the driveway were no longer my own.

I stopped on the concrete as the ambulance came bounding around the corner.

Where are you going? I silently screamed at them. For a fleeting moment, I wondered if I'd imagined it, if perhaps the ambulance really was headed somewhere else. But my heart knew the truth. I waved my arms frantically, beckoning the EMTs back, but they drove farther and farther away from us instead, away from my dad, away from the place they needed to be.

I pumped my arms up and down until they burned, trying in vain to catch their attention. I would have shouted if I'd had any air left in my lungs. Looking up, I silently screamed at the ominously sparkling stars, now clear in the sudden darkness.

Oh, I thought in a trance. *Those stars would have been perfect for stargazing.*

Another ambulance rumbled past the front of the house, and I stumbled back up the sidewalk to meet it. The driver stopped by our apple tree and leaned out the window, yelling, "I can't see the house number! Is this the right one?"

"It's here!" I yelled. Then, in a whisper: "It's here."

I stood there on the sidewalk, my legs shaking, as the paramedic bounded out and followed me inside the house.

Mom was sweating, panicking, pumping her fists into my dad's chest again and again.

"He's not breathing! He's not breathing!" she gasped. Her entire body was shaking. My dad's belly shook as my mom performed CPR on him. His eyes—oh, his eyes were open, and they were looking up, but they couldn't see anything.

(Where was he during all of this? What did he see? Where did he go?)

More paramedics bounded in, one after another—the other ambulance must have made it back to the house. I blinked, and suddenly there were too many people in our house, setting up equipment and calling out orders.

An EMT took my mother's place. Mom picked up her phone, still on the line with 911, and ended the call. It had taken them roughly ten minutes to arrive.

I stood by my dad, watching his bulging eyes staring out at nothing as the paramedics tried to make his heart start again. I heard a horrible gurgling noise come out of his mouth, one last strangled breath wheezing out of his lungs.

This wasn't my dad. This wasn't the fortress I knew.

I held my mom close as she murmured into my neck, "He's not breathing, Gabrielle, he's not breathing, oh my gosh, what do we *do*, he's not breathing."

I stroked her hair and soothed her quietly.

"It's going to be okay," I said. "It's okay. He's okay."

I was not afraid. I had not and would not process the enormity of the situation.

ONE BREATH AT A TIME

Not as we stood there. Not as my dad choked on his last breath. Not for days, or weeks, or even months.

It was faith, I decided in that moment. It was my steadfast, immovable faith. I knew not only that God could fix my dad, but that He was *going* to do it. We would get to keep him. He would start breathing again. He would live.

There was never a doubt in my mind.

God Will Let Us Keep Him

Emergency responders checked my dad's vitals and jammed tubes down his throat. They ripped open his sugar skull shirt, that shirt he loved so much, right down the middle. They pumped air into lungs that no longer remembered how to breathe.

The paramedics asked Mom about Dad's health.

"High blood pressure," she murmured, letting go of me and tugging on her hair. "And diabetes. Type two."

Mom hunted for Dad's medicine in his closet. She finally came back out with a list of his medications for the EMTs to refer to. Then she retreated to her closet. I didn't know why—I thought she was still looking for medicine. In reality, she had left because she could not bear to watch the paramedics do everything they could do and have it still not be enough to save her husband.

But I stayed. I didn't know what else to do. I stood frozen between the kitchen and the living room, watching the paramedics pump my dad's body with air.

They tried defibrillators. My dad's arms and legs shot out as electricity surged through him. A frog in a science experiment.

Does that hurt? I asked in anguish. *Are you still in there, Dad? Can you feel that?*

The question was not if he would come back. The question was when. How long will this take? How long will it be before his heart starts again, before his eyes blink again, before his lungs take in a shaky, renewing breath of air?

Your ribs are breaking, I trembled. *If you're in there, you're hurting. Oh my, you must be hurting.*

My primary anguish then was the unanswerable question of whether my dad was in pain. I craved the comfort of knowing that he was not experiencing this pain, that he was no longer hurting or afraid. My mind raced, trying to soothe itself.

People have heart attacks all the time, right? They're survivable. And the paramedics got here SO fast. Mom was right there to do CPR. She was right there! He's going to be okay. He's going to start breathing again, and we will smile at him and squeeze his hands as they take him out the door to the hospital. We'll go see Dad in the morning when he wakes up. He'll be in a hospital bed with tubes running all over. It will be scary, but at least he'll be okay. We'll gently hug him and tell him we love him. It will all be okay.

Mom finally returned from her room, crying and hyperventilating, interrupting my frenzied train of thought. As she came to stand beside me, I let out a whimper I'd been holding back.

"Can I hold his hand?" I whispered. "I just want to hold his hand. Would I be in the way?"

"I think you would be," she choked. "I'm so sorry."

Mom pulled me into the dining room. We knelt on the rug together, holding each other, and whispered the most fervent prayer we had ever uttered. Reverently, repeatedly, we murmured these words: "Oh, let us keep him. We need him here. Let us keep him. Please, please, please. We need him. We need him here."

God hears righteous prayers, and he answers them, I thought with confidence. *God will let us keep him. My dad is going to live.*

My idea of faith stemmed from the notion that those who are trying their best will have their wishes met—that if I believed hard enough, I could make my hopes a reality. If things didn't go the way I wanted them to, it was my fault for not believing hard enough.

(I had so much to learn.)

(I still do.)

We rose to our feet and returned to the living room, but Mom turned away from my dad.

"I can't watch this," she whispered, scrunching up her eyes. Then, raising her gaze to meet mine, she asked in wide-eyed desperation, "Oh, what do we do about Kenji?"

"I'll take Sam and go pick him up," I offered. It was almost 9:00. "You can stay with Dad, and when they go to the hospital, you can follow them. I'll go take care of the boys."

She nodded and sent me out. I wonder, now, if she knew then that he wasn't going to make it, and she just didn't want me to be there for it. I wonder why she thought she had to be that strong, why she thought she had to bear that alone.

But at the time, I didn't question it. I had a task to accomplish, something to do besides watching my dad's body be

ONE BREATH AT A TIME

bruised and broken, and I was going to do it. I grabbed Mom's car keys, hoisted Sam onto my hip, and made my way out to the garage.

Donna, our neighbor and my high school art teacher, stood in the driveway in her pajamas.

"What can I do?" she asked. "Do you need me to go get Kenji?"

"No, no," I said. "I can do it."

Then, as I pulled out onto the street, I stopped.

"Actually, I need you. Please come with me," I said. Donna hopped wordlessly into the passenger seat, and I drove away.

I left the car running in the driveway with Donna and Sam inside and went inside to find Kenji. There were kids crowded all around the dining room table as the birthday girl opened her gifts.

"Hey, Kenji!" I said, forcing a smile onto my face. "We need to go, hon!"

While Kenji put on his shoes and complained about having to leave so early, I made small talk with the host. She asked if everything was okay. I said all was well, we just needed to get Kenji home.

(I wasn't lying. I was positive that everything would be okay.)

We were on Yamashita Bridge heading home when an unrecognized number called me. It was 9:16 p.m.

"Hello," said the soft voice on the line. "Your mom doesn't want you to come home. You and the boys can come to my house for a while."

"Oh," I said, stopping at the edge of the bridge. "Who is this?"

"Oh, I'm sorry, I should have said. It's Lisa," she told me. It was the bishop's wife. My friend Grady's mom.

"Okay," I said. "Okay, we'll be right over."

We carried the boys into the house. Lisa turned on an Avengers movie for my little brothers and led them to a bin of toys in the living room. I didn't know why the bishop wasn't in there with us. I would later learn that the bishop was at my house, cradling my father's head in his hands, giving him a priesthood blessing.

But I didn't know that. I didn't know how serious things were. Back at the bishop's house, I alternated between sitting and standing and pacing, but nothing felt comfortable. I was stuck inside my head.

The paramedics are going to get Dad's heart started again. They will take him to the hospital, and Mom will go with them. I will stay with the boys. Mom will call from the hospital. We will go see them. It will all be okay.

This was all a bad dream. Reality would set in again, and he would be okay. I was sure of it. There was no other way.

Mom called me at 9:29 but immediately hung up. I would later learn it was at that exact moment that the paramedics called it. It had been about an hour. It wasn't working. Dad was gone.

Other neighbors and family friends showed up at the house. I don't know if my mom collapsed. If she wailed. Who held her.

It was 9:29. He'd been gone for about an hour. He was gone when Mom started trying to save him.

ONE BREATH AT A TIME

    I pictured his glassy eyes staring upward, seeing nothing. Seeing everything.
    I called her back at 9:30, but she didn't answer.
    I didn't know.
    I didn't know.

Nothing but Hope

Our friends Shanan and Becky came over just after 10:00 p.m. and told me that Mom wanted me to come home. Donna volunteered to stay with the boys and the car.

It was pitch black outside now. I climbed into the back seat. It only took about five minutes, but it was a long, quiet ride. We were almost there when a sliver of reality crept into my view. I finally asked, in a tiny voice, "Is he gone?"

"What?" they asked. I had said it too softly.

Louder, the sinking feeling in my stomach growing heavier, I asked, "Is my dad gone?"

"That's something you need to talk with your mom about," said Shanan.

This isn't right. This isn't right.

But still caught in a trance, still pinching myself awake, I thought that he was alive. I thought he would be okay.

Mom was standing in the driveway when we pulled up. She pulled me to her.

"They tried," she whispered. "They did everything they could. But he's gone."

It hit. A tsunami of sorrows. My breath caught in my throat.

No, no, no. This can't be happening.

ONE BREATH AT A TIME

Two police cars and two ambulances were parked on the street, and a helicopter rested in the field across the road. Everything was turned off. Sitting quietly. Too quietly. No one was trying anymore. It was over.

"It's not your fault," she murmured. "It's not your fault."

I hadn't considered causation until that moment. But my obsessive-compulsive disorder heard those words and latched onto them with a vengeance. My mind began spiraling. The thoughts came in a rush, like floodwaters into a valley.

You're the reason he's not alive, my OCD said. *You took him on a run. His heart couldn't handle it. It's your fault.*

Was this really all because of me?

My head spun. How could I ever live with the horrible reality that I had done this to him? Maybe it was my OCD confusing me, but maybe it was real. I didn't know yet that PTSD would add to that equation, conspiring with OCD to compound my confusion about what had really caused Dad's death, making my stomach churn forever afterwards. The line between reality and anxiety blurred. How could I have done this?

"You don't have to go see him until you're ready," Mom whispered, calling me back to the present moment. "Are you ready?"

I wasn't ready. I never would be. But I nodded, nonetheless, and stepped, shaking, towards the door. It was only a few yards, but it felt like miles as I trembled forward, my legs buckling beneath me. The porch light shone an ugly shade of yellow-brown in the darkness. I didn't remember it being that color before. I did not look at the faces lining the stairs as I passed them—a friend of my mother's, then a police officer.

Their hands reached out for me, and I walked through them. Through the doorway.

Oh, Dad!

A sob tore through me as I entered the living room and saw the sheet covering everything but his face. His stomach was distended unnaturally from all the air the EMTs tried to force into him. There was still a breathing tube jammed down his throat and sticking out of his mouth.

I knelt by my dad's body and looked at him, really looked at him. I reached forward and stroked his soft black hair. There was a distinct smell on his skin already, something earthy. It frightened me.

What are you supposed to do when this happens? I wondered. I tried to remember what characters in movies and books did when tragic things happened. *What would I do if I were one of them? What would I do if this weren't real, if this were all just a story someone made up?*

Slowly, I slipped off my pink running shoes, the ones Dad had picked out for me, and put them neatly by the stairs. Mom sat by my father's head, her back against the couch, as I reached tentatively for my father's hand. It was still warm. Soft.

My body was not my own. I picked my legs up and laid myself mechanically beside Dad. I was crumpling, the way paper does when you feed it to a roaring fire. It curls in on itself, charring, flaking. That was what was happening to my soul.

I looked at his sweet face. I took in the freckles splashed across his nose and cheeks, freckles just like mine. I saw them clearer than I ever had before. The meticulously plucked black eyebrows and soft eyelashes. Lips stuck inside a breathing tube. His soft face.

"Why is there blood?" I whispered. There were flecks of blood across his face, tiny droplets sprayed over his cheeks and eyelids. "Why is there so much blood?"

"I don't know," Mom trembled.

"His hand," I choked up. "He just keeps getting colder."

I stroked his soft hair as tears began blurring my vision. Mom went and pulled out a blanket of his, a sushi-print quilt she had sewn for him years ago. She covered me with it, and I lay there, falling apart, wrapped in my father's memory.

"Oh," Mom finally whispered. "We have to tell Taylor."

Taylor. I swallowed. My twenty-year-old brother was on a Church mission in Salem, Oregon. It was late—he would have been in bed already. I lay there on the floor, eyes squeezed shut, holding Dad's cold fingers, as my mom called Taylor and whispered to him that Dad was gone. I imagined him sitting up slowly, bending over in shock as the words registered.

We were expecting Taylor home in July. It had been almost two years since he had seen his father. And now he wouldn't see him again. Not in this life.

I couldn't fathom that horrible reality. I watched Dad's stomach and could have sworn I saw it moving. I watched his lips, waiting for him to breathe, waiting for him to inhale again, for the paramedics to come back in and say, "Oh, he was there all along!" Lazarus came back from the dead. Dad could, too.

But there was nothing I could do. Nothing but hope. I lay there, praying, "Dear Heavenly Father, I love you, but I do not understand . . ."

I just kept lying there, holding his hand. That's all I'd wanted to do while they were working on him. I just wanted to hold his hand. I would have been in the way, but there was nothing they could do, anyway.

I just wanted to hold him. I just wanted to take this away from him.

People tried to bring me pillows. They stroked my hair and asked if I wanted to sit or stand. If I was comfortable. But none of it mattered.

I felt that I would never be comfortable again.

The Hardest Part

*It turns out, the hardest part
isn't watching him die.
At that point,
You're still in shock.
It doesn't quite set in, even as you lie there
And hold his hand.*

*It's living after. It's reliving those
nightmare moments
And trying to put the puzzle
pieces back together
After they've been mangled, chewed up,
Spit out.*

*It's crying out to God and asking
If there's another way.
It's learning to accept, finally,
That His is the only way.*

*It is learning to ask God
To hold you. To keep you. To make you better.*

*"I cannot carry this on my own," you whisper.
And He replies, "You do not have to."*

Light

This is my soul
Cracking.
This is the gaping
Raw wound
Where you used to be,
Where your memory
Still lingers.

But maybe this crack
Is where the
Light comes through.

Maybe this chasm
Is where my Savior
Comes in.

Garden

The first twenty-four hours were the hardest.

It is now in my memory only in snapshots—

It is close to midnight, and we are telling Kenji what happened. He is crying in our arms, sinking to the floor in the dim light of the kitchen.

I am lying awake in my mother's bed. 1:00 a.m. 2:00 a.m. 3:00.

Daylight. I am lying on the floor in my friend Aubrey's living room, and she is stroking my hair as I cry, my tears running down her leg.

There are people at our house cleaning the blood out of the carpet (why, why is there so much blood on the carpet?). They can't get all of it out, so we'll scrub at the stain for weeks, as if by cleaning it up we can clean up that night, make it go away, make him come back.

I read *Saints* chapter 45, which chronicles the reactions of Joseph Smith's family after his martyrdom. His mother, Lucy Mack Smith, asks, "My God . . . Why hast thou forsaken this family?"[1] I feel peace in knowing that I am not alone in this suffering, that I am not the only one who loves God and still feels abandoned by Him.

---

1. Lucy Mack Smith, History, 1845, 312–13.

Relatives fly in from Washington.

I spend a lot of time on the floor, falling apart.

And finally the sun hides itself again, and I pick myself up off the floor, and I realize that it has almost been twenty-four hours. I have survived this awful day by taking it one breath at a time. I have almost made it.

But there is a night ahead of me I cannot face alone.

I called my friend Reanna and whispered into the phone that I needed her to come over and spend the night with me.

Minutes after I crawled into bed, she arrived. Reanna climbed in next to me and held me while I shook and cried. Another friend, Ashlynn, showed up soon after. I was sandwiched between friends. They said soothing things, then let me ramble, and then they told me funny stories. It felt strange to laugh again. The sound echoed in my hollowed-out soul.

It was late. I watched the clock, my stomach full of rocks, as it hit the twenty-four-hour mark. I was exhausted yet relieved. I had made it through one day. One. Whole. Day. I exhaled, letting the weight of the world exit my body.

My friends on either side of me talked less and less and gradually drifted off to sleep. I lay there, wide awake, stuck in the middle, as my friends rested. I could not sleep. I was alone in my thoughts.

I am in the Garden of Gethsemane, I thought with a thread of disappointment, *and you are asleep.*

It was a thought that came not out of anger but out of sadness. We read in Matthew 26 that Christ brought friends with Him but ultimately could not take them into the garden. He had to face that portion of His journey alone.

"And he cometh unto the disciples, and findeth them

asleep, and saith unto Peter, What, could ye not watch with me one hour?" (Matthew 26:40).

Lying there in the darkness between my sleeping friends, I understood Christ's pain, if only an inkling of it, for the first time. I felt His pain in being let down—"What, could ye not watch with me one hour?" Could you not stay awake with me as I lie here and cry?

But verse 41 explains, "The spirit indeed is willing, but the flesh is weak."

Peter, like my friends, was willing to watch with Christ, yet he succumbed to sleep. What matters, then, is that he came with Christ at all—that when Christ told him of the immense pain and sorrow He was about to take upon Him, that Peter came with Him, and waited.

He was with Him. He did not enter the garden, but he waited outside. He showed up. He cared.

My friends stayed there with me that whole night. They bound together my eggshell pieces and made me whole.

"Thy friends do stand by thee, and they shall hail thee again with warm hearts and friendly hands" (D&C 121:9).

Reanna and Ashlynn did not enter the garden with me. I had to fight through the grief and the anguish for myself. That burden was mine to bear. My friends waited outside the garden. They hailed me with warm hearts and friendly hands.

And that was more than enough.

God Shall Wipe Away All Tears

Grief feels a lot like a car wreck.

I barely had the energy to get out of bed, let alone to shower, to wash my hair, or to make myself eat. To force myself to keep living.

Sunday came. It had only been just over twenty-four hours, and no one expected me to go to church. Yet I could not shake the feeling that out of all the efforts I could make, all the ways I could try to heal, going to the house of God was what I was supposed to do.

Reanna and Ashlynn slipped out of bed in the morning and drove home to get ready for church. I met them at the chapel just as the opening hymn started, slipping into the back row with a friend on either side of me.

A hush fell over the congregation as the sacrament was passed. Tears welled in my eyes and ran down my cheeks. My whole body ached with a deeper sorrow than any I'd ever known. Silently, I cried out to Heavenly Father.

"God, I cannot do this. I do not have the strength to do this," I told Him. "Please take this away from me. Please take this for me. This is a burden I do not know how to carry."

Then, as clearly as if they had been spoken from the pulpit, these words came to my mind: "God shall wipe away all tears" (Revelation 21:4).

Where are you, God? I asked Him in anguish. *Where are you to wipe away my tears?*

The moment I offered up this prayer, I felt hands touching either side of my face.

Reanna and Ashlynn, prompted only by the Spirit, were gently wiping my tears off my cheeks.

I didn't quite process the majesty of that act as I sat there in sacrament meeting. The ceremony of the sacrament transitioned to neighbors and friends standing at the pulpit in solemnity and bearing quiet, fervent testimonies of life after death. I was caught up in the stories they shared of my dad's Christlike example.

"I know prayer works," a young girl testified. "And I know we can pray for the Shiozawas, and they are going to be okay."

"I'm not just going to talk about Troy, because that's not what sacrament meeting is about," a man trembled. "But I am going to talk about the way I saw Christ in him."

"I know God will wipe away all tears," said a friend. There it was again. God promising to wipe away my tears.

Where are you? Where are you to wipe them away?

Later that night, the words ran through my mind again. I was nestled on my living room couch with my friends Aubrey and Abby on either side of me. We were looking through an album of family photos.

God shall wipe away all tears. A quiet, distant murmur.

I flipped from one photo to the next, my heart breaking over and over again. I wanted to drink in every snapshot, to remember everything I could about my sweet dad. I wanted to hold him in my heart.

Tears ran down both cheeks once again. Before I could lift a hand to wipe them away, I felt my friends' hands on either side wiping them away for me.

It was then that it finally struck me that God *was* there with me, wiping away my tears—He was just there in the form of my friends. He was Reanna and Ashlynn in sacrament meeting. He was Aubrey and Abby in my living room. He was, and is, in every good person and every good act that will ever take place. He was right there beside me.

"This is my glory, that perhaps I may be an instrument in the hands of God," says Alma (Alma 29:9). "This is my joy."

We are meant to be used by God. We are instruments in His hands. We are serving in His name, preaching in His place, sharing His word—

We are sitting by our friends as they cry. We are wiping away their tears until there are no more tears to wipe away.

I Am Here

Dad began having problems with his vision in December 2018. A blood vessel burst in his left eye one night. Another night, another blood vessel burst in the same eye. This painful ordeal made him almost entirely lose his vision in that eye, caused severe headaches, and limited his hand-eye coordination.

In *A Farewell to Arms*, Ernest Hemingway writes, "You are so brave and quiet I forget you are suffering." That is how I regarded my stoic father as he battled. He hardly let anyone know what he was going through.

The worst was yet to come. He was subjected to surgery after surgery, painful procedures that brought him to tears, wrecked his vision, and then slowly began to heal him. He described these procedures as "a handful of needles in my eye." It was excruciating to see him like this.

After a particularly grueling surgery on May 1, 2019, baby Sam was playing with my dad and head-butted him, hard, in his left eye. Dad slipped my brother from his arms with a quiet groan, and he covered his face in his hands, doubling over in pain. He stayed like that for several minutes, leaning on the back of the couch, wrapped in anguish.

I rested my hand on his back and asked gently if there was anything I could do to help him.

"No," he whispered, his voice strained, as he held his tormented head in his hands. "No, nothing."

There is an unparalleled ache to watching someone suffer and not being able to do anything to alleviate his pain. All I could do for my dad was stand there beside him and rub his back while he suffered. I could only say, "I am here, I am here. What can I do?"

Taking a nap with Dad at age 1, April 2002.

Sometimes we can't do anything. Sometimes we just have to be reassuring witnesses to the unraveling of one's psyche, of their very soul cracking.

I cannot end your experience, Dad. I cannot take away your pain, I thought. *But I am here, and I will be here still. I will hold your hand as you fight your way out yourself.*

Two days later he was gone.

In that same spot on the living room floor where he had bent over and held his anguished head, that exact same place behind the couch where he'd leaned for support, he fell and never got up.

Lying on the floor beside his body the night my dad died, I looked around and realized how perfect that lesson was that I had learned just two days before. I'd learned that there is no perfect response to other people's suffering. There is no perfect scripture reference to memorize, no perfect dessert to ease their pain, no perfect hug that can cure their ills. But the greatest gesture of all is not to have the perfect offering, but to be perfectly willing to offer help. The best thing of all is just to say, "I am here."

There was a tenderness to the fact that even if no one could change the way we were suffering in the wake of my father's death, there were countless people who came to our aide. They brought meals that couldn't heal us but that filled our stomachs. They gave hugs that could not bind our eggshell pieces together but could give us the strength to make it one more hour. They said, "I'm here if you need to talk" and "Take all the time you need to get that essay turned in" and "I'm willing to help in any way that I can."

That's really all we can ask for. That's all we can really give another person. We reach out a loving hand and a willing heart, and we say—"I am here. I am here. I am here."

The Purest Form of Love

Monday came, and I knew I couldn't go to school, but I did the one thing that I thought I could handle at that point: I went to seminary. I knew that I needed to be close to the Spirit, to people who cared about me, to people who cared about Christ. I knew I wanted to be within the walls of church buildings as much as I could.

When I showed up at the church, Brother Holyoak pulled me into his office. This was no ordinary seminary day, my seminary teacher explained; we were taking the semester exam that day, but I didn't have to participate.

I was crestfallen. I had wanted to come sit back and enjoy a lesson on my Savior, to dive into the Doctrine and Covenants, to learn, feel the Spirit, and hear the testimonies and insights of my classmates.

I felt bitter that my effort in coming to seminary had been in vain.

It wasn't in vain, though. I knew that, even in my disappointment. I was still here, still inside the church building, still surrounded by the quiet reassurance of the Spirit. Brother Holyoak and I stayed in his office for a while, and he talked with me.

He asked me the questions no one else had yet: What

was I doing to deal with this trial? What actions was I taking? Where was I turning?

I told him I'd been reading the scriptures and *Saints*, that I'd gone to church, that I was taking my time healing and learning to let others serve me in a way I never had before.

I don't remember much about the conversation. I remember discussing a portrait of Christ that hung on his shelf, a pencil sketch of the Savior with a crown of thorns on His head. I remember, most of all, that my dear seminary teacher just sat with me. That he testified of Christ. That he validated my pain. And, finally, he said words that stuck out to me so much that I wrote them down that very day, that I dated them so I'd always remember when and why he'd said them.

"Gabrielle," said Brother Holyoak, looking me in the eye, smiling softly. "Mourning is the purest form of love."

I let his words wash over me, and I knew instantly that they were true. It wouldn't hurt this much if I didn't love him this much. I wouldn't ache like this if I didn't care.

When my classmates finished their assessment, they filtered into the office, one by one, and sat around me, and hugged me, and stayed with me until it was time to go. They told stories to make me laugh, drew goofy pictures on the whiteboard, and offered their support and love.

In that tiny office that day were my classmates, my teacher, and an undeniable spirit of truth, of comfort, of love. And then there was me. Still stuck in the aching and the mourning. Yet knowing, deeply, that this was the purest form of love I knew.

Haunted House

The so-called "five stages of grief" are discussed as a linear process, as if opening one door immediately closes the previous. In my experience, however, this could not be further from the truth.

My mind is a haunted house with doors that intermittently open and close, depression dropping in on denial, anger paying acceptance a visit. It is a fun house of mazes and mirrors . . . without any of the fun.

There are days when I laugh. I ride my bike through my neighborhood and feel fresh air on my skin, and I smile. I collect freckles. I buy new shirts. I listen to music and laugh so hard my stomach hurts.

But there are far too many days filled with another kind of ache, a complete draining of the senses. It is an exhaustion that is not cured by sleep, a pain that is not cured by medicine, a tossing, back-and-forth anguish that cannot be soothed, not by company, not by any balm.

There is a perfect Thanksgiving one year and a heartbreaking one the next. Halloweens hit me with unexpected gut punches as I recall the fun we used to have together that we can have no more. I find solace in my hometown some days and on others cannot bear to be in Moapa Valley, to live where he died, to drive on the roads where that nightmare evening turned my life upside down.

These are the floor days, the I-can't-do-this-anymore days. These are the days when, sobbing, I ask God if there is no other way, but say, "Nevertheless not my will, but thine, be done" (Luke 22:42).

It is a hard thing to ask. It is a hard thing to accept His will without knowing.

Yet it is the only thing I have left on those floor days. It is the only thing that gives me strength: turning my will over to His, accepting that He knows more than I do. Accepting that He can give pain purpose when I cannot.

This is a stage of my life I did not expect to walk into. It is a stage of growth and intense loneliness and a deep reliance on my Savior. As I explained it to my friend Abby in early July, "It's only been two months, and it seems like the rest of the world has moved on, but there's a fresh reminder and a new ache every single day. I'm learning a ton, and I'm trying to be patient, but it's definitely the hardest—and most spiritual—my life has been."

"It's not cool what happened," Abby said, "but it's cool how you are able to grow from it."

Grief is the roommate I didn't ask for, who barged his way in and burrowed under the covers and wouldn't move back out. Grief is the one who stole my food and tracked mud through the living room. He's the one who sewed a permanent gray storm cloud over my head.

But grief is also my greatest teacher. He has shown me who to keep in my life and who to show the door. What to value. What to let go of. How to live better and drink more

deeply from that bitter cup. How to wrap my hands around a
new kind of joy I never knew before.
    I didn't ask for you, Grief. I didn't invite you in.
    But I welcome you here. I welcome this growth.
    Because I am now in the cocoon, working, growing—
    And at last, when I emerge, it will mean something.

Bodies

"Did you feel that?" Taylor whispers to me. "The spirit's different. He's not in there anymore."

It was May 9, the day before Dad's funeral, and we were gathered at the mortuary for a private family viewing. I carried an anvil of anxiety about seeing him this way, but I still expected him to look like himself—red-faced, bright, and happy. I thought it would look like he was asleep.

The anxiety I felt magnified into full-blown nausea as the mortician rolled the cart that held my dad's body into the room, as I took in what had become of my dear father's body.

He was gray. Yellowish gray.

He was stiff, too. I hadn't been ready for that. A paper cutout of the man I knew.

I fought back a sob as the mortician settled my dad's cart in front of us. Mom, Taylor, and I helped put the remaining details of the temple clothes on his body. As we gently lifted and turned him to secure the sashes around and beneath him, I was struck by how light he was, how hollow.

That body is not my dad, I thought. *That body is not who he is.*

Once my dad was fully dressed and his body was settled into the coffin we'd picked out, all the family members who'd been waiting outside—Dad's parents, his siblings and their children, my mom's parents, and little Kenji and Sam—came into the room, and we all took turns coming to my father's body. Beholding him. Speaking to him. Kissing him.

I am still gutted by the gnawing memory of my little cousins' wails. By watching my grandpa, my dad's dad, sink defeatedly into a chair. By the sight of my dad in that coffin, one step closer to being put to rest in the earth.

And that was when Taylor leaned over to me and put into words what I had not been able to explain—that the spirit of the room was different because Dad simply was not in that body anymore.

It had served its purpose for this lifetime. It was done, retired, finished. I imagined a weight lifted off my father's shoulders. No more pain. No more surgeries. No more exhaustion. I looked at that body that was no longer my father, and I thought of peace. Of rest. Of a life that is more than this.

Our family at Dad's funeral in May 2019.
From left: me, Kenji, Sam, Mom, Taylor.

But I thought, too, of the imperfections of mortal bodies. Of what had happened to my dad's forty-eight-year-old home: Hypertensive cardiovascular disease.

That's what it says on the death certificate. That's how they define the moment my dad's heart stopped beating.

Type-two diabetes. High blood pressure. Years upon years of inadequate sleep and elevated stress levels.

Stubborn. Strong. Not wanting to ask for help. (And I wonder where I get it.)

I cannot even imagine the exhaustion, the toll that forty-eight years of wear and tear could have on a body.

I take after my father in so many ways, from our endless freckles and broad shoulders to our insomnia and love of adrenaline. But what other similarities lie beneath the surface?

After examining the way my dad lived—and the way my dad died—my OCD threw me into a panic over the state of my own body. I began compulsively checking my blood pressure, the state of my kidneys, my blood sugar. Biking as fast as I could, as often as I could. Avoiding any foods that seemed "scary." The struggles of post-traumatic stress disorder were compounded when the tight-chested anxiety I felt reminded me that bodies weren't as trustworthy or as invincible as I thought they were.

Am I eating too much junk food? I asked. *Am I avoiding exercise too often? Am I staying up too late and getting up too late and doing too little to manage my stress?*

Am I stressing about this stress too much?

How much of this is genetic? How much of it is environmental?

Will I, just like him, be gone before my fifties, lying on the living room floor, leaving a family behind to mourn?

Deeply burdened by my questions, I turned to a variety of sources, the most promising of which were the scriptures. In Doctrine and Covenants 89, I read about the revelation of the Word of Wisdom, which was received by Joseph Smith in February 1833. We are promised there that all who follow this commandment "shall receive health in their navel and marrow to their bones . . . and shall run and not be weary . . . and the destroying angel shall pass by them, as the children of Israel, and not slay them" (D&C 89:18–21).

How I want that for my dad! I thought. *How I wish for him to still be here, to be healthy, to run without weariness, to have the destroying angel pass him by. I ache for him!*

I kept reading. Just ten months after Joseph Smith received the Word of Wisdom, in December 1833, he received another revelation. This time, Saints in Missouri were being persecuted and driven from their homes. Their belongings were taken, their crops destroyed, their lives threatened.

In the midst of this turmoil, as the Saints fretted over these threats of death and destruction, they were comforted by these words from the Savior: "Fear not even unto death; for in this world your joy is not full, but in me your joy is full. Therefore, care not for the body, neither the life of the body; but care for the soul, and for the life of the soul" (D&C 101:36–37).

"Care not for the body"? I couldn't believe it!

I thought back on everything my dad had done during mortality. My father cared more for the well-being of others than he did for his own life. How selfless he is! He sacrificed sleep, relaxation, and his own wants to answer the call of duty. He was a wonderful leader at work, an outstanding bishop, a loving friend and father and neighbor.

"Seek the face of the Lord always, that in patience ye may possess your souls, and ye shall have eternal life" (D&C 101:38).

I look around now at all the people my dad helped in more ways than I can imagine. I look around, and I see what really happened—that my dad cared for his soul more than his body. That he sought the face of the Lord. That he will have eternal life.

I do not panic as much as I once did over the state of my body, but there are still plenty of days when I find myself feeling troubled. Part of that struggle simply stems from the reality of living in a fallen world. Elder David A. Bednar explained, "Because a physical body is so central to the Father's plan of happiness and our spiritual development, Lucifer seeks to frustrate our progression by tempting us to use our bodies improperly."[1]

Satan is miserable because he does not have a body. Thus, he wants us to be miserable because we do have bodies. One of the greatest errors we can make is letting him convince us that our bodies are less capable and less worthy than they truly are. He tries to make us take the focus away from what really matters: how we use the precious gift of our bodies to serve others.

So now, as I contemplate how my dad lived his life and think about how I want to live my own, I worry less about what my body looks like and less about its faults. Instead, I think more and more about how I can use what I have to serve others. Who I can lift, hug, and serve. Whose lives can be touched by mine.

"While we may all want to know the secret to a long life, I

---

1. David A. Bednar, "We Believe in Being Chaste," *Ensign*, May 2013.

often feel we'd be better off devoting more time to figuring out what makes a good life, whatever span we're allotted," Elder D. Todd Christofferson taught.[2]

I believe what we ought to learn from facing mortality is that we are such frail and imperfect creatures, and that we ought to delight in that! We treasure our bodies as the gifts they are, at the tangible representation they are of our agency. We use our mouths to smile and give friendly greetings. We use our hands to serve and lift each other up. We use our legs to run to the aid of others, and we use our arms to hold them.

---

2. D. Todd Christofferson, "Sustainable Societies," *Ensign*, November 2020.

Let Love In

I have never enjoyed asking for help. If there's a homework problem I don't understand, I will stew away at it for hours before taking it to anyone for guidance. When I broke my thumb in fifth grade, I waited until it turned swollen and purple several days later to tell my parents what had happened. And it took me more than a decade of silently struggling with my obsessive-compulsive disorder—whose favorite tactic was to make me doubt I was sick at all—to finally be clinically diagnosed at age seventeen and begin pursuing treatment for the disease that was taking over my life.

But losing my dad was an unprecedented experience of debilitation. His death was the flood that broke my walls of resistance—walls of stubborn pride, self-deprecation, and fear of vulnerability. Suddenly, in those agonizing moments, all I wanted was to let others in.

It was a foreign feeling. But here were community members and friends and peers reaching out, saying they'd be there if I needed any help.

You know what? I finally thought. *I* DO *need help.*

I knew I could wallow on my own or try to trudge along the way I usually did when I was struggling. But I had finally, truly, hit rock bottom, and I knew without a doubt that the only way I was going to get out was by climbing on my friends' shoulders to get back into the light.

So I called friends I hadn't talked to in some time to drive me to class, stay the night, or help me study. I texted peers in my seminary class to come sit by me so I'd feel more comfortable. When my neighbor Jen asked if there was anything she could bring me, I asked her to buy me some oranges, because that was the only food that sounded appetizing.

I let them in.

I let them help.

I finally realized this fundamental truth: It is just as important to let ourselves be loved and served as it is to love and serve others.

Before my father's death, I always preferred to be on the serving end. I still do. But if I do not let others serve me, I am denying them that same kind of joy I experience when I get to serve.

"When you attempt to live life's experiences alone, you are not being true to yourself," taught Elder Robert D. Hales. "It has been said that no one is so rich that he does not need another's help. . . . The disposition to ask assistance from others with confidence, and to grant it with kindness, should be part of our very nature."[1]

Along with making it possible for more blessings to be added upon others, letting ourselves be served allows us to be more open to the love and blessings God is waiting to bestow upon us. President Spencer W. Kimball said, "The Lord does notice us, and he watches over us. But it is usually through

---

1. Robert D. Hales, "We Can't Do It Alone," *Ensign*, November 1975.

another person that he meets our needs.[2]" By refusing the help of others, we are refusing the aid of our Heavenly Father.

I finally came to understand that in order to let people fulfill their baptismal covenant to "mourn with those that mourn" and to "comfort those that stand in need of comfort," I needed to let those people in (Mosiah 18:9). I had to let them serve me. I had to let them know I was mourning before they could mourn with me.

I didn't need those walls of resistance to be safe. I didn't have to be afraid of asking for help, and I no longer had to give in to the narrative that I was not worthy of asking for help. I never had to earn the service of others or prove myself worthy of it, and I never should have turned it away.

It turned out that all I needed was to let love in.

---

2. Spencer W. Kimball, "President Kimball Speaks Out on Service to Others," *New Era*, March 1981.

Speed Limits Don't Exist Anymore

It was the day after what would have been my dad's forty-ninth birthday, and I was still trying to recover from that emotionally devastating day. I had planned to travel to St. George with my friend Aubrey and her family that morning, but I awoke feeling like the weight of the world was still pressing me down, and I canceled at the last minute.

There was a wrenching pain in my gut.

You're a horrible friend! I told myself miserably. *You committed to going, and she was just trying to be nice. How dare you.*

The person I was from one minute to the next was changing so rapidly that I could hardly keep up with her. The person I was when I had made plans with Aubrey was not the same person that woke up the next morning and canceled them. That person was different from the one who existed that afternoon, and even more different from the one who slept in my bed that evening. I was trying to plan a future for someone who didn't even exist yet.

My limbs felt heavy. I took my time getting ready. I listened to some inane pop music to drown out my bitter thoughts. I couldn't listen to anything I'd heard before because those old songs meant old memories. "Cecilia and the

Satellite"? Pink Floyd? Forget it. Everything reminded me of Dad.

I decided to run some errands. I drove ten minutes to the post office, leaning back with my wrists draped over the steering wheel. Driving suddenly felt boring and monotonous. In this feverish state, I glanced at a speed-limit sign, and I decided that speed limits sounded like mere suggestions.

Why do they even exist? I thought. *Do they even matter?*

I'd sped before, maybe five miles over if I was late to school. But not regularly. Not insanely.

But this wasn't my normal self. This was my PTSD self, even if I hadn't been diagnosed just yet and didn't understand quite what was happening to me. This was the version of myself with the angry emotions and flashbacks and pains she didn't know how to cope with. This was not the optimistic Gabrielle who had celebrated her bittersweet high school graduation or even the angry Gabrielle who had visited the cemetery on her Dad's birthday. This was a Gabrielle who didn't care anymore.

I left the post office with a new thought running laps through my mind: *Speed limits don't exist anymore.*

Why should they? I'd never been pulled over before. Everyone else seemed to speed, too. Why did it even matter? Thirty-five miles per hour was way too slow, anyway.

So I pressed down on the pedal, watching the road instead of the speedometer, speeding up around the curve. Forty-five miles per hour. Fifty.

I was usually watchful for police cars when I was on the road, but this one looked like any other vehicle. Black and sleek, heading the opposite direction from me. But it wasn't just any other car: It was a well-disguised cop car.

Well played, state trooper. Well. Played.

I didn't process what was happening or how fast I was going until the red-and-blue lights started flashing like a disco across the front of the officer's car. He screeched to a stop and spun around to tail me.

What kind of cop car has lights like that? I wondered. There was no bar across the top, no red, white, and blue, like I was used to. *Maybe I'm actually in* Tron. *Or maybe this is a dream.*

So, you probably know this, but you're supposed to stop if a police car flashes his lights.

But I am nothing if not naïve.

Maybe he'll let me go, I thought in a trance. *After all, we're in the fifty-five zone now. And I'm going, like, fifty. Please accept my changed behavior and just let me go.*

I wasn't even sure how fast I'd actually been going. Ten miles over? Twenty? Could it really have been more than that?

In retrospect, the smart thing to do to quell my uncertainty would have been to pull over. Even if the policeman hadn't been chasing me, at least I could have gotten out of his path.

But I chugged along for a good half mile while he sped up behind me, tailing closely, siren blaring. Reality set in at last, and I veered off and slammed my brakes in the gravel along the side of the road.

I sat with my head down and my heart racing.

"Roll down the back window!" the officer barked. He had short, stubbly blond hair and a round face covered by a thick pair of black sunglasses.

"Why didn't you stop?" he demanded.

"I don't know! I don't know," I exhaled, putting up my hands. "I . . . I guess I didn't realize at first. I'm sorry."

"But why didn't you stop? Didn't you see my lights?"

"They . . . didn't look like they normally do? I was confused," I babbled. "I'm sorry."

He yelled an incoherent instruction at me through the open window, but he might as well have been speaking Greek. I didn't process anything he'd said. I knew to pull out my license, though. My hands shook as I rifled through my wallet.

He screamed at me again. "NOW!"

"I'm trying to find it, I'm trying, I'm sorry," I said, tears blurring my vision.

"License, registration, and insurance!" he shouted.

Was that what he had been saying? My hands shook as I rummaged through stacks of papers in the glove compartment.

"Um. This?" I held up the vehicle registration.

"Yes, that's the registration," he mocked as he took it from me.

I peeled a few more papers apart and found the insurance card. I still wasn't sure if that was what he had asked for, but it seemed right.

He walked back to his car and stayed there for what felt like agonizing hours but was probably only ten minutes. I sat with my head turned away from the road in shame, hoping no one would recognize me or my car.

Heavenly Father, I'm so sorry, I cried. *I'm embarrassed and I'm sorry and I'll be better. I don't know why I'm like this. I don't know who I am right now.*

I thanked Him that it wasn't worse and asked Him to keep me safe, because I was still terrified.

But I'm so sorry, I prayed. *I don't know why I can't get through these feelings. I don't know why I did that. What's going on with me? Who am I?*

The officer finally swaggered back over to the car. He held out the ticket and explained the number I'd have to call, the fine I'd have to pay, and how it would put a point on my license if I didn't take traffic school.

I swallowed.

He gave me a warning, too, "for yelling at him," and told me it would be worse if he pulled me over again.

I didn't yell at you, I thought bitterly. *You were the one yelling at* me. *I was just trying to figure out what you were saying.*

He finally left me there in the dust. I rolled the windows up and sat there, devastated, catching my breath. Tears rolled down my cheeks. I swallowed hard.

I waited until the officer was long out of sight before I put my turn signal on and shifted back onto the road. Slower now. I was only a mile away from home.

Nothing feels real anymore, I thought. *I still don't know how fast I was going. I'm floating, floating.*

Maybe this was my brain's way of protecting itself. It was convincing me I wasn't really there, stuck in all these messes. This unprecedented nightmare. My brain was dissociating from everything happening in my life so I wouldn't have to feel it so deeply. I was floating.

But I am still here.

I pinched myself awake, but all it did was leave a bruise.

I am still here.

There is no getting out of this.

Life Lessons from the Grand Canyon

When it's been less than a month since you've lost a loved one, you're emotionally and physically drained, and all you want to do is sleep until the years have melted away. It's probably not the best idea to try to muster up the energy to hike the entire Grand Canyon, rim to rim, let alone do it in a single day, sunup to sundown.

Yet my mom and I did it. Our friends headed down the canyon armed with walking sticks and CamelBaks, and we went right along with them.

Hiking the Grand Canyon was something my mom had wanted to check off her bucket list since forever.

Hiking the Grand Canyon was something I had never, ever wanted to do.

I don't know what I was trying to prove to myself by hiking it. I was inadequately prepared, exhausted, traumatized, and struggling to see the good in anything.

Yet it was there, swallowed up in the Grand Canyon, that I found myself. It was there that I began to heal. I learned valuable lessons in the canyon—lessons that would sustain me, and continue to sustain me now, through this journey.

⨯ Life Lesson #1:
When you are discouraged, just look back at
how far you've already come!

There were so many times while hiking the Grand Canyon that I looked ahead of me and felt defeated, overwhelmed, by the miles of rocky ridges I had yet to conquer. I felt daunted by the challenge I'd undertaken. How could I keep going? How could I ever make it?

Yet when I looked behind me, I saw majestic ridgelines growing distant. I stared back in amazement at the miles I'd already hiked, the progress I'd already made. I had already traveled so far—what were a few more miles? What were a few more steps?

And what if there was incredible joy and beauty to be found, even in the pain of my journey?

There have been so many times along my winding road to healing that I have become angry and defeated.

So many painful months have already dragged by, I'd think bitterly. *I'll never make it out of this.*

But when I look back, I see all the lessons I've learned so far, all the miles I've already traveled, all the love I've gotten to feel. There is still a lifetime of ridges to climb—that is true. But I have already made it this far into the canyon. I have leaned on my trekking poles—my Savior. He has led me this far. He will not leave me alone.

I have miles to go before I can rest.

But I have already made it farther than I ever thought I could.

ONE BREATH AT A TIME

✕ Life Lesson #2:
If ye are prepared, ye shall not fear!

"There's water at the head of the trail, right?" Mom and I asked.

Our friends looked at each other, then back at us.

"No . . ." they said slowly. "We brought our own. We don't know how long it will be before there's water again."

Mom and I were like the virgins in the parable who were unprepared to meet the bridegroom because they hadn't brought enough oil for their lamps. We searched the car for water bottles and found enough to fill our CamelBaks halfway, which was enough to set us off on our journey but was not enough to sustain us until the end. We'd have to find more water as soon as we could.

In healing from grief, there have been so many days when I have wanted someone to hold me but been too exhausted and afraid to ask. Instead, I have prayed for them to come hold me, for some angel to come feel my pain with me so that I did not have to suffer alone. There have been so many days of quiet loneliness and bitter desperation. There have been so many empty CamelBaks with no wells in sight and unlit lamps with no oil to fill them.

Sometimes, I give myself permission to feel sorry for myself. But more and more, rather than pitying myself in these moments, I am learning to prepare instead. When others offer their help, their love, their time, I make a note of what they are willing to share. I let them serve me. I call them and ask them to come sit with me, distract me with a fun adventure, or help me study for tests when I don't have the energy to do it on my own. These moments fill my CamelBak enough that I can set out into the canyon again. These moments give me just enough light to keep going.

But I am learning, too, to be prepared for the moments when no one is there.

When it's the middle of the night and you're sweating through a flashback, but you don't want to wake anybody up. When you text your classmates to ask them to help you study for a big test, and they say they'll be there, but then none of them come over. When the hurt is too heavy to bear on your own, but no one else should have to be burdened with your sorrow.

I am preparing for these moments by leaning on my Savior. By telling Him, *I'm lonely, I'm hurt, I can't do this on my own.*

You see, God gives us more than we can handle alone. But He does not give us more than we can handle when we lean on Christ. "For he maketh sore, and bindeth up: he woundeth, and his hands make whole" (Job 5:18).

There is hurting, and there is healing. Because of our Savior, there is purpose, and even peace, in our pain.

I did not come into the Grand Canyon with enough water to drink, but I found more along the way. I leaned on the support of others. And I drank from the Living Water as I trekked deeper and deeper into the canyon. I found His light along the way.

When we come into the Grand Canyon with breathable clothing, water and snacks, and shoes that fit us well, we do not have to fear the hot summer sun. When we prepare for the journey, we do not have to fear the miles ahead of us. We are ready.

When we come into grief with supportive friends, faith

and hope, and a loving relationship with our Heavenly Father, we do not have to cower in fear. When we hold strong to what we know to be true and good, we can set off into the canyon, rejoicing.

"If ye are prepared, ye shall not fear" (D&C 38:30).

We still may not know for certain what awaits us in the canyon, what kind of struggles we will face, how hard the journey will be. There are still times when it seems we are walking entirely on our own. But we know who is traveling alongside us, bearing us up, and carrying us whenever our trials are too cumbersome to hold on our own.

"I will go and do," we say, like Nephi (1 Nephi 3:7). We prepare as well as we can.

And we trust that God will carry us the rest of the way.

⨯ Life Lesson #3:
Address molehills before they become mountains.

They weren't my hiking shoes.

But the label said they were my normal size, and even if they seemed a little snug when I first tried them on, they weren't *too* tight . . . and at least I knew they'd never fall off my feet. The fact that our friends had happened to have that extra pair of shoes in the first place and the fact that they happened to be "my size" were miraculous enough that I didn't want to question it.

Hiking roughly twenty-four steep miles in ill-fitting shoes isn't a good idea. That was my first mistake.

But even worse than setting off on the trail in those shoes was the fact that I ignored the horrible discomfort that came with wearing them. I gritted my teeth, I fought through the pain, I assumed it would go away.

Halfway through the canyon, exhausted from limping along, I finally stopped at a picnic table and peeled off my socks. Gaping red blisters were forming between my toes and across my heels. My feet, rubbed raw with dirt and sweat, pulsed with open sores and red-hot pain.

Mom lent me some clean socks to change into, and I slipped on a couple of Band-Aids, but it was already too late. Instead of taking preventative measures, like stopping at the head of the trail and wrapping my feet in duct tape when they had first started hurting, I had ignored the pain until it got too bad to bear.

The pain only grew. As we trekked in the darkness along the final miles of switchbacks, I gritted my teeth and pushed against my walking sticks, trying to make my way up yet another hill.

Suddenly, I cried out as I took a step and felt a fat blister burst open, white-hot, between my toes.

I could have worn more trustworthy shoes or made frequent stops along the trail to care for my feet. Instead, I ignored my pain until it was almost unbearable, and I paid for that mistake for over a month after the hike until my feet finally healed.

But blisters weren't the only kind of pain I was choosing to ignore. The Sunday before we hiked the Grand Canyon, I walked into our home office, and Mom looked up from her computer with a furrowed brow.

"I think you have PTSD," she said.

Earlier that day, as she sat on my bedroom floor, Mom

ONE BREATH AT A TIME

told me that she didn't remember much about the night my father died, that it had all become a blur to her.

"I remember too much," I responded, shaking my head.

I hadn't even told her about the flashbacks, about the all-consuming horror of reliving those moments over and over again. I hadn't mentioned the erupting irritability and impatience I felt at the smallest things, how everything in my body felt like a live wire, or how everything from sirens to the smell of pizza triggered an emotional reaction for me. I hadn't told her about how my mind had captured that night so perfectly that I could replay it, almost word for word, moment by moment, on command.

Yet here Mom was at the computer, trying to diagnose me with an internet search.

At first, just like ignoring the pain in my feet, it was a lot easier to pretend that everything was fine than it was to peel off the socks and take a look at what was really going on in there. It was a lot easier to keep pushing through, even when it was excruciating, instead of facing the molehill—instead of facing what my life had turned into.

But finally, when I could limp along no farther, I had to face the truth: time doesn't heal all wounds. It's what you *do* with that time that matters. I had to accept that as untouchable as I aspired to be, one cannot have a frame of reference for something they have never experienced before. Every grief is unique. Every loss brings a different wave of pain. More walls broke down within me until I conceded to seeking treatment outside of my own efforts. And eighteen months after losing my dad, I was finally diagnosed with post-traumatic stress disorder.

Gently exploring the unknown, I found that in grieving

and growing, I was not stepping blindly. Instead, I was walking by faith. I was trusting in my Savior. I was trusting in the power of "line upon line, precept upon precept." I was taking tiny, brave steps into the unknown.

Some of that unknown was the PTSD diagnosis I had never expected to deal with. Some of that uncertainty came from new ways that my OCD reared its ugly head in response to my new trauma. There were new challenges to deal with, both in the inner workings of my mind and in the changing circumstances around me, that I had not anticipated.

I couldn't ignore those tight, aching shoes. I had to face those wounds.

So I wrote. I wrote about the things that hurt and the things that healed, captured my journey, untangled the knot in my stomach.

I sought my Savior more fully. I asked the hard questions about the gospel, and I received my own answers.

I started talking about my dad more and sharing the story of May 3, 2019, even thought it was bitter and painful. The more I talked about it, the less it hurt me. Little by little, I peeled away those aching layers and bandaged them with healing words.

I went to therapy despite my every inclination to avoid it, trying as many different therapists as it took to find the right fit. I told one counselor about the aftermath of losing my dad, how exhausted and afraid I felt, how I was still carrying around the heavy burden of quietly mourning.

He looked up at me.

"My dad died when I was in high school, too," the counselor said. "I know what this feels like."

ONE BREATH AT A TIME

I find more and more people who know what this feels like. We build a network of love and loss and healing. In reliving this trauma again and again, it lessens its power over me. If this is what "normal" looks like now, I am embracing it. The more I expose myself to these things that I fear, the braver I become.

I am leaning on friends and family. On leaders and therapists. On people who can let me rest from my grief, who help me to keep from developing more blisters, who provide balms to soothe the wounds I already have.

Most of all, I am learning to lean on God. I am giving Him my molehill so that it does not grow any higher.

Instead of ignoring my pain, I am owning it. I am facing it. I am conquering it.

It cannot control me any longer.

⌧ Life Lesson #4:
Seek light.

When the going gets rough
And everything aches, and
You cannot take another step

Look up.

To the stars. To the finish line
To headlamps ahead.
To others who have made it
Before you, have traveled
That lonely road and drunk
The bitter cup.

GABRIELLE SHIOZAWA

You focus on Christ
And aches ease.
Light increases. And
Life
Gets
Better.

You will make it out
Of the canyon.

You will look back at others
Who are starting out
On their journey.
You will reach out your hand
And say—

"I've been there, too.
I know
It's dark.
But I promise—

There is light.
Not only on the other side
But now,
Even here,
Even where the night
Seems darkest.

Look up."

ONE BREATH AT A TIME

✕ Life Lesson #5:
When you cannot handle looking to the end
of the road, just look a few feet ahead of you.

There is power in looking to the far rim of the Grand Canyon, in believing you have the energy and willpower to make it all the way to the other side. There is power in looking to the eternities and in believing in good things to come.

But in the minute-to-minute withering from pain and grief, when you are struggling to make it through the day and are too exhausted to take another step, it is agonizing to look to the future. The edge of the canyon looks like mockery instead of like a promise.

So, instead of focusing on how far I have left to go, I take it one day at a time. One moment at a time. One breath at a time. I'm stumbling along the dusty Grand Canyon trail, ready to give up, but I focus on the tiny footsteps I am taking forward. I point my flashlight a few feet ahead, and I keep walking. I walk as far as I can see, and I shine the light of the gospel a little bit ahead, and I let it guide my feet. I'm learning that I don't have to see the whole trail. I don't have to know how rocky it's going to get or how high I'm going to have to climb. I just have to know it's there and that it's worth it and that my aching legs can make it farther than I think they can.

These are the small steps. These are the tiny tender mercies. These are the ways we keep going.

"Don't you quit. You keep walking. You keep trying," said Elder Jeffrey R. Holland. "There is help and happiness ahead. Some blessings come soon, some come late, and some don't come until heaven; but for those who embrace the gospel of Jesus Christ, they come."[1]

In the Grand Canyon, I was traveling uphill, in darkness, on a road I'd never taken before. I was exhausted. Blistered. Worn out.

I knew I'd reach the rim of the canyon eventually. I knew that there would be a day when my grief would be only a faint scar instead of a gaping wound. I knew I wouldn't hurt like this forever.

But it was the little things that kept me going. The tiny stream up ahead promising a cool drink of water. The friends by my side. The strong muscles in my thighs and calves encouraging me to climb higher, higher, higher.

So I decided not to worry about the mountains I had yet to scale. I was on the right path. Even if I had to stop to rest sometimes, I was headed the right direction. I could deal with the summit another day.

Christ taught, "Take therefore no thought for the morrow: for the morrow shall take thought for the things of itself. . . . Your heavenly Father knoweth that ye have need of all these things" (Matthew 6:32, 34).

He provides us with daily sustenance to help us grow. He supports us as we work to climb through the canyon.

One step at a time, one breath at a time, we will make it.

---

1. Jeffrey R. Holland, "An High Priest of Good Things to Come," *Ensign*, November 1999.

ONE BREATH AT A TIME

✕ Life Lesson #6:
When we focus on our progress instead
of our aches, we hurt less and have more joy.

Hiking the Grand Canyon is a feat I am proud of. It is a resume-builder, a character strengthener, a mark that I could do something daunting, even amid one of the hardest trials of my life.

Yet I quickly found that the more I focused on how much it ached—how tender the skin on my palms was from rubbing against my walking sticks, how agonizing the blisters were on my raw, burning feet—the more exhausted and angry I felt. The more I focused on my aches, the more those pains seized me, churned within me, until they were all I could focus on.

In the midst of this pain, I decided to start focusing elsewhere. I observed the blue sky above me and the red canyon walls rising up around me. I took in the waves of greenery growing unexpectedly amid the dry desert—cacti, bushes, and trees. I saw life and growth, an endless collage of gorgeous mountain peaks and canyon ridges stretching out ahead of me and behind me.

It was beautiful.

When I focused on the lovely nature that surrounded me, on the sweet friends I had with me, and on how much progress I had already made, I found great joy in my journey. I skipped, ran, sang, laughed. I drank in the experience deeply, and I loved it.

But gradually the pains started growing more acute, demanding to be felt . . . and I gave in. I began to slow down, to complain, to grumble. I stopped focusing on the good, on my progress, on the incredible journey I was on, and instead zeroed in on my pain, my discomfort, and the bitter sorrow I had carried with me into the canyon.

Sadness and grief are necessary, and even beautiful, parts of our mortal journey. Our moments of greatest anguish can be our most effective teachers. There is nothing wrong with feeling those difficult emotions—it is a vital aspect of being human.

Mom and me at the Grand Canyon, June 2019.

But we do not have to stay here, in this anguish, forever. President Russell M. Nelson taught:

> My dear brothers and sisters, the joy we feel has little to do with the circumstances of our lives and everything to do with the focus of our lives. When the focus of our lives is on God's plan of salvation, which President Thomas S. Monson just taught us, and Jesus

Christ and His gospel, we can feel joy regardless of what is happening—or not happening—in our lives. Joy comes from and because of Him. He is the source of all joy.[2]

This journey is going to hurt, but it is also going to be beautiful. You are going to experience unprecedented joy. The pain is going to be worth it. You will reach the end and look back at all you've accomplished, all you've felt, all you've gained.

So focus on Christ. Your aches will ease. The light around you and within you will grow brighter. Your life will become better.

You don't think you can make it through this pain. But you can.

You are going to be so proud of who you become.

---

2. Russell M. Nelson, "Joy and Spiritual Survival," *Ensign*, November 2016.

Salvation

There was one more powerful lesson I learned in the Grand Canyon, one more insight for me to carry out with me, but it was one I hadn't expected in the slightest.

Daylight was fading as I rested beside my mom on the side of the trail. With some trepidation, Mom shared with me what was weighing her down: unresolved mistakes Dad had made before he died.

I didn't realize that I had expected my father to be perfect until I found out that he wasn't. It broke my heart. As I grappled with this new knowledge over the following months, I felt burdened by all my unanswered questions. *Is my dad good enough? Is he going to make it?*

Months went by, and I was still deeply struggling. I just wanted to know that my dad would be okay, that he wouldn't have to suffer, that all the good he had done in his life would counteract the instances when he faltered.

I didn't realize how much guilt I was still carrying about my father's death or how much anxiety I still had about his salvation until I finally broke down in tears in Relief Society one Sunday and couldn't stop. I couldn't understand where it was coming from at first. I just knew I was overwhelmed.

But then, as I was sitting there at the back of the room

wiping away my tears, I felt a clear prompting come to me: *Go. Talk. To. The. Bishop.*

I don't need to talk to him, I argued, nauseated by the thought. *That's terrifying. I don't want to go talk to him.*

Yet it came again. *Go. Talk. To. The. Bishop.*

As I begrudgingly made my way down to his office after church, I trembled with anxiety. I wasn't sure how to say what I needed to say. Finally, the Spirit overcame me.

I started by telling my bishop how guilty I felt for taking my dad on a run that night when his heart couldn't handle it.

"You weren't trying to stop his heart; you were trying to prolong his life!" my bishop exclaimed. "Please don't feel guilty about that anymore. It was not your fault."

It wasn't my fault? As the Spirit confirmed the truth of this statement to me, I was overcome with the most powerful relief and peace I'd felt in a long time. My OCD slithered away, if only for a moment.

I kept going. I confided in my bishop how worried I was about my dad. I just wanted to know if he was okay.

My bishop told me that he had worried about his father, too, when he passed away, and how he himself struggled with a lot of temptations. We talked for a while about how the Atonement works on both sides of the veil and how merciful God is.

Finally, my bishop looked me in the eye and said, "Gabrielle, I'm giving you permission not to worry about him anymore. Just love him. Write down the things you remember loving about him. Forgive him if you need to. Remember all the good he did, and don't worry about his salvation anymore."

Almost immediately, the weight I had been carrying began to lift off my shoulders.

He's okay, I thought. *He's going to be okay.*

"God is so much more forgiving than humans are," my bishop said. "It will all work out."

We sat in silence for a long time. Then he said, ever so softly, "Gabrielle, I feel prompted to tell you that you are good and that you are forgiven."

A wave of relief washed over me. As I floated back out of the church, tears streamed down my face once more, but this time from joy instead of pain. I felt lighter than I ever had before.

It is not our job to declare a verdict on our fellow men, alive or dead. It is not our place to even worry about their salvation once they have passed through the veil. Instead, we have the peace of knowing that the only one allowed to judge us is a loving God who wants the best for each of His children. Joseph Smith taught, "While one portion of the human race is judging and condemning the other without mercy, the Great Parent of the universe looks upon the whole of the human family with a fatherly care and paternal regard."[1] Our Heavenly Father is first and foremost a parent, and He wants us to come home to Him.

✕✕

Reading through notes my dad left behind, searching for consolation, I am touched by how often his thoughts turned to repentance and humility.

---

1. Joseph Smith, in Joseph Fielding Smith, *Teachings of the Prophet Joseph Smith* (American Fork, UT: Covenant Communications, 2005).

ONE BREATH AT A TIME

"My regrets and shortcomings are magnified as I see my children, and I long to help them have more by avoiding the pitfalls that ensnared me," Dad wrote. "I want them to find joy without the pain, but that isn't the plan."

He left other notes: "A righteous man continually repents." "Repentance is not a punishment, it is a blessing."

He spent so much time working on improving himself, and he always encouraged his children and others under his stewardship to do likewise. Even the last talk he gave in church, an address he delivered to the local singles branch on April 28, 2019, was about repentance and worthiness. A girl in the congregation later sent me the following message about his talk:

"He talked a lot about worthiness and how we all make mistakes, but Heavenly Father and Christ still love us, no matter what. I will never forget his analogy that even if a hundred-dollar bill is torn or worn or stepped on or crumbled or anything like that, it still has the same worth as a crisp, new hundred dollar bill. And that's how Christ and Heavenly Father see us. . . . No matter if we are torn or take the wrong path or make a mistake, we are still worth the same to them. They love us no matter what."

I later found more notes that my dad had written about the analogy of the hundred-dollar bill. "In life, you will often feel desperate, poorly treated, or hated by others. You will feel worthless. But be aware that no matter what pain you go through, misery you feel, or how many people push you away, you will never lose your value to those who love you. Even if you aren't rich or have nearly nothing, you will never lose your value."

Why did he focus so much on worthiness? Was he ashamed by the things he lacked? Could he not see all the things he did right?

I know I'm not the only one who has been burdened by wondering whether the choices of their family members will inhibit the eternal progression and unity of their families. But to myself and to anyone else who frets over this uncertainty, President Henry B. Eyring taught, "You are worrying about the wrong problem. You just live worthy of the celestial kingdom, and the family arrangements will be more wonderful than you can imagine."

I look at my dad as a whole work of art—a patchwork of love and joy, faults and struggles, hard work and compassion. I look at all the good he did, and I look at him, and I think, *If I love him this much, how much more must my Heavenly Father love him?*

And if I forgive him, won't my Heavenly Father forgive him, too?

I do not worry about his salvation anymore.

Opposition in All Things

"I'm grateful for opposition."

I looked up in surprise. A classmate stood before our group with quiet power, in his white shirt and tie, bearing his testimony.

It was June 2019, and we were in the Sacred Grove in Palmyra, New York. Some high school seniors celebrate their graduation by taking cruises to Mexico or flights to Paris, but a large portion of my graduating class took a tour to see sacred sites from Church history instead. We started with a flight to Kansas City, Missouri. From there, we took a tour bus all the way up to Fayette, New York, making plenty of stops along the way. It was the perfect way to seal our testimonies with spiritually enlightening experiences before we set off into the world on our own.

As we sat in the Sacred Grove that Sunday, the light came filtering through the trees, spinning everything around us into gold. My peers and I sat quietly as we witnessed each other's testimonies being borne both silently and aloud.

My classmate explained that if there was no darkness, we would never see the stars. If not for Satan fighting against Joseph Smith in the Sacred Grove during the First Vision, encircling him in darkness, the light of our Savior would not have seemed so brilliant in contrast.

I found his words surprising at first, but as I mulled them over in the days to follow, it became more and more apparent to me just how right he was. I realized that I, too, was grateful for opposition. I am grateful for the contrasts that show me the goodness of God.

"For it must needs be, that there is an opposition in all things. If not so . . . righteousness could not be brought to pass, neither wickedness, neither holiness nor misery, neither good nor bad," Lehi taught. Without this opposition, he said, we would have "no life neither death, nor corruption nor incorruption, happiness nor misery, neither sense nor insensibility" (2 Nephi 2:11).

The reality is that the mortal experience would have no meaning if we did not die. We would have no urgency, no drive, if we expected to exist in this state forever.

I would not know how to feel joy, I thought in wonder, *if I did not have to experience this sorrow, too.*

Doubts are a chance for us to reaffirm to ourselves what we know to be true. Grief is the way we learn just how deep our capacity is for love. And facing a chaotic world each day, even with uncertainty looming ever-present on the horizon, is a new opportunity for us to learn how to become more like God.

Job was a great example of exercising faith in the face of opposition. Satan scourged him with "sore boils from the sole of his foot unto his crown" (Job 2:7). His wife, incredulous as to how Job could remain so humble amid this affliction, asked, "Dost thou still retain thine integrity? Curse God, and die" (v. 9).

I understand her disbelief. How exhausting it must have

been to watch her husband suffer. Why should we keep believing when, despite our efforts, hard trials still come our way? But I love Job's eye-opening response.

"Thou speakest as one of the foolish women speaketh," he reprimands. "What? Shall we receive good at the hand of God, and shall we not receive evil?" (v. 10).

We spend so much time asking God for what we want, begging for people to be healed, for good things to happen, for our lives to go the way we want them to.

Yet He has already given us so much. We have this entire beautiful world to enjoy, and everything in it. We have our talents, our ambitions, our frailties, and our strengths. We have the messy and beautiful experience of being human. We have Christ to heal us. And we have each other to love.

What more can we ask for?

Peter writes, "Beloved, think it not strange concerning the fiery trial which is to try you, as though some strange thing happened unto you: But rejoice, inasmuch as ye are partakers of Christ's sufferings; that, when his glory shall be revealed, ye may be glad also with exceeding joy" (1 Peter 4:12–13).

When we suffer, Peter teaches, we are experiencing a minute facet of what our Savior went through in Gethsemane—we are learning a human-sized portion of what it means to become like God. In submitting to sorrow, to trials, to pain, we are also allowing ourselves to be subject to the joy and glory of our Savior.

Are we going to receive all this goodness, then, to bask in the promise of eternal light and joy and glory, and still ask for more? to refuse the bitter cup? to say, *no, I refuse to suffer, I refuse to face opposition and grow, I refuse to let life be what it is meant to be?*

What if we stopped asking God to do what we want Him to do, and instead allowed Him to be who He is, to exercise His power in the way He sees fit? What if we trusted that He knows what is best for us?

Putting Down the Kickstand

When I was seventeen and tired of running, I decided to get my old bicycle out of the garage, dust it off, and start riding it again. Almost immediately, I was filled with a great sense of exhilaration. Why would I run ever again when I could go coasting down the highway with the breeze in my hair?

My rose-colored vision was soon tarnished, however: Bugs kept flying into my eyes, and my knees hurt like never before.

The first part was a pretty easy fix: wearing sunglasses on my bike rides kept the bugs away *and* made me look ten times cooler (or so I thought).

Fixing my knees wasn't quite as easy. It took some research and some trial and error, but I finally figured out that my technique wasn't quite what it could be. Fortunately, I took a break before things got too bad with my knees. Once I knew what the problem was, I could address it, one step at a time. Being conscientious about my bicycling form—and alternating my rides with some good old-fashioned running—helped solve what had before seemed so burdensome.

It had annoyed me to have to take a break from what I loved, but I soon realized how much better off I was for having done so. Soon, I was back on my bike again, flying around town—albeit with greater caution and better technique.

One day, as I rode far from home, up a series of hills, my bike started choking up on me. I looked down and realized that my chain had slipped off. Undeterred, I tried slipping the chain back on, changing gears, riding backwards—you name it. All to no avail.

Finally, I looked around and processed just how far from home I really was. I had no clue what I was doing, and there was no way I was walking my bicycle all the way home. Defeated, I put down my kickstand.

A Father's Day card I'd once made for my dad came to mind. On the front I'd written, "If at first you don't succeed, call Dad."

Dancing to Chubby Checker's
"Let's Twist Again" at girls' camp, June 2018.

"Fine!" seventeen-year-old me huffed. "I'll call Dad."

I didn't have to wait long before my father came rolling up

ONE BREATH AT A TIME

towards the mesa in his white Dodge. He had a large cup of cold water for me to sip while he set to work fixing my bike.

The ease with which my dad fixed my bicycle seemed like magic. Something that had frustrated me, made me sweat, and nearly driven me to tears was something that my dad, with all his knowledge and experience, could easily solve. At that moment, I was filled with a rush of gratitude. Not only was I so grateful to have a dad like mine—I was grateful that I'd been able to get over my hubris and just give him a call!

Life, like bicycling, requires momentum. Once we get going, we don't want to brake for even a moment, let alone put down the kickstand! Albert Einstein is quoted as having said, "Life is like riding a bicycle. To keep your balance you must keep moving."

While I'm loath to contradict one of the greatest geniuses ever born, this statement must be examined. There are many times in our lives when we have to put down the kickstand, step back, and take a look at our bicycle—and at ourselves. Pushing mile after mile with a flat tire will put unnecessary strain on your bike as well as on your body. Maybe your chain has slipped; your gears might be faulty; you could have tendonitis or muscle soreness from overuse. Perhaps there's even a greater underlying injury that hasn't yet been detected, and maybe the bicycle itself has to be scrapped. Whatever the case, it does us well to take a break and properly figure out what the issue is if we want to be able to move on successfully on our ride.

Losing my dad wasn't an ordinary ache. It wasn't a type of soreness that could be cured with more exercise. It was debilitating. It wasn't just aching knees or a chain that slipped off my bike. This was broken bones and smashed handlebars. And unlike my situation with my bicycle, my dad was nowhere in sight to help.

As much as I wanted to keep trucking along, to be stronger than what was tearing me down, I was broken. My grief and trauma forced me to slow down, to rest in bed, to listen for the Spirit. They made me close my eyes, take a deep breath, and put down the kickstand for a while.

Even though I resisted at first, I finally accepted that it is sometimes necessary to take a break. You have to talk to a therapist or a doctor and see if you can heal what has been broken. You have to gather the courage to call your dad to come help you fix your broken bike or your Heavenly Father to help you fix your broken heart.

Eventually, I got back on the bike. Social events slowly got easier. I had small amounts of energy once again for running, hanging out with friends, and going about my normal, everyday ativities. There was still pain, but this time it wasn't so much agony as it was the pain of growing. When biking, the tightening of your calves and the burning of your lungs as you push uphill isn't a sign to give up: Instead, this pain is a sign that you're working, that you're growing—that you're living!

But I'm so grateful I put the kickstand down for a while. I'm so glad I started asking for help. I'm so glad I rested.

Sometimes, taking a break—and reaching out—is an act of bravery in itself.

White Butterflies

One warm summer day in Moapa Valley, I took my little cousins Stella and Lulu for a walk along the railroad tracks behind my house. We skipped, competed to see who could balance on the railroad ties the longest, and picked sunflowers along the edge of the tracks to tuck behind our ears.

As we made our way towards a large patch of sunflowers west of the tracks, Lulu pointed out a kaleidoscope of pearly white butterflies emerging from deep within the cluster of blossoms.

"Look! White butterflies," she said. "My teacher told me when you see a white butterfly, it's someone you love that died."

Lulu paused a moment.

"Hey, maybe it's Uncle Troy! Hi, Uncle Troy!" she said, waving at the butterflies.

I watched the tiny white wings flutter up into the blue.

And I smiled.

Just as those white butterflies made Lulu think of her Uncle Troy, that summer I started seeing signs of my father everywhere I looked. But I wasn't always sure whether it was a blessing or a burden.

On our church history trip after graduation, my peers and I made a stop in Ontario to see Niagara Falls. As I laughed and reveled in the glory of the falls, I thought, *Oh, I have to tell Dad about this when I call him tonight! He'll love it.*

But immediately an anvil dropped in my stomach as I realized what I'd forgotten in that tiny moment, and I ached all over again.

Later that night, exploring Ontario and trying to find a good place to eat dinner, we came across Coca Cola World. A bittersweet wave of emotions came over me again as I stepped into that red-and-white checkered wonderland of Coke products and fancy ice cream sundaes. A panic began to rise in my throat. My breathing turned shallow.

I want Dad here to see this, I thought in anguish. *He would love this. Oh, how he would love this. I want to take him here. I wish I could get ice cream with him and I could photograph his big, happy smile because he would love this with his whole heart, and because I love him with all of mine . . . Oh how I wish he was here, here, here . . .*

It wasn't until we were back in the tour bus driving away from Coca Cola World that a realization finally came into my heavy heart:

Dad put Coca Cola World there.

Not literally. But we could have dropped by somewhere else on our tour. We could have gone to Niagara Falls on the American side instead of in Canada, or we could have gone to a different part of town for dinner, or we could have driven home from another direction.

ONE BREATH AT A TIME

But we stopped at Coca Cola World. That was no coincidence. Dad could not be there with me to experience it physically, yet I truly know that he was there with me in that moment, saying, "Here I am, Boo. Here I am."

I think he knew I'd stop and look at it, that it would hurt in the moment, but that later I would look back at that shop, at that imaginary snapshot of him, and I would smile.

And I do, Dad. I do. I'll worry less now about whether you're here in person to experience these wonders with me. I'll revel instead in how many white butterflies fill my life because of you.

✕✕

A few weeks after that trip to Niagara Falls, I was sitting in a restaurant in Lindon, Utah, just before closing when the song on the radio suddenly changed, catching me by surprise.

"Let's Twist Again" by Chubby Checker! It was Dad's song!

There was a girls' camp lip sync battle where he and I boogied to this beat. There were countless nights when he danced to this song in the kitchen. Endless trips where he played it in his truck and sang along, bopping his head to the beat and grinning ear-to-ear.

I put down my sandwich on the diner plate, and a tear rolled down my cheek.

Dang it, Dad, I thought miserably. *I miss you. I miss you. I miss you. I want to dance with you. I want your laugh filling up the kitchen again because I'm starting to forget what it sounded like.*

But as much as it hurt me at first to hear that song, I

soon realized what a sweet white butterfly that moment was. Because I know that one day these memories of him dancing and singing will be years and years in the past, and all I will have is this remembering. This beautiful remembering of dancing with Dad and watching him live. My skin cells will change and grow, and someday soon I will have skin cells on my arms that have never wrapped my dad in a hug, but at least these brain cells will remember.

And through that remembering, Dad will keep living.

In these white butterflies and these tender moments, he lives and lives and lives.

✕✕

At dinner one night in June, Sam asks through a mouthful of noodles, "Where Troy go?"

(He is so used to hearing my mom call Dad by his first name that he refers to him as Troy more often than as Dad.)

Mom sniffles and turns away from him, leaning on the edge of the kitchen sink. "He's gone, honey. He's gone."

Sam takes another bite and furrows his brow.

"Troy hurt?" he asks.

(How much did he remember from that night? How much was his two-year-old brain capable of processing?)

"Yeah," Mom murmurs. "Troy hurt."

Sam returns to his dinner. But we know it will not be long before more questions come, some we can answer and some we cannot.

A month later, after making little-to-no mention of Dad in all that time, Sam thinks of him again.

"Where's Daddy?" he asks late one night.

ONE BREATH AT A TIME

Mom pauses.

"He's with Heavenly Father," she answers.

"No, he's not," Sam argues.

"No? Where is he?" Mom asks.

"He's home," Sam says.

"What? Where?" she asked, playing along.

"Closet," Sam says. "In his closet."

It's true, I think. I find him in his closet in his cleanly organized shirts and his starched jeans. I find him in the smells of his hair gel and his cologne.

I find him in temples, especially in the baptistry, as I remember the countless times we performed baptisms for the dead together. How we left the temple, hand-in-hand.

I find him in the chapel where he presided as bishop and in the office where he worked and in the truck he spent so many hours driving.

He is not in his coffin. I do not find him at his graveside. I find him everywhere else, instead. I find him in his favorite movies and in every new restaurant I try, in the handwritten notes he left behind and the music I hear on the radio. I find him everywhere, everywhere, everywhere.

He is here.

Nudging me along. Showing me how to love.

Showing me, in death, how to live.

I travel to places I haven't gone with Dad, but everywhere has something that makes me think of him. At an airport in New York, I pass a man in an ASU shirt, and I remember how much he loves their mascot, the Sun Devil. I wander through an antique shop in Hannibal, Missouri, and find his reflection in a set of ceramic Coca Cola polar bears. I see him on sugar skull shirts in Cozumel just like the one he wore the night he died. He's talking excitedly to the owner of a tabasco shop in New Orleans and is eating his favorite clam chowder with me at Pike Place in Seattle. He's the Coca Cola trucks we pass in San Francisco and a delicious burger shop we eat at in Provo, and he is in every white butterfly I see.

And finally, finally, I can see these ever-present white butterflies, these endless reminders, as a gift instead of a burden.

I'm so grateful I can't forget him. I'm so grateful that everywhere I look, I see the life and color he infused into everything he touched. All the love he put into this world. All the white butterflies soaring by.

It makes me love you even more, Dad, I think.
And that love drowns out almost all the aching.

Father's Day

I dreaded the first Father's Day, knowing what a torrent of emotions it could bring.

And it was painful, just as I expected. But it was so much more than that. It was a day of miracles, of kind words, of soft hearts. It was a day of my dear friends, my loving Heavenly Father, and love for my sweet dad.

I awoke to an email from my friend Morgan, who was serving a Church mission in Rome, Italy. She told me her mission president, whose father had died when he was around my age, advised her to record things she loved about my dad and then share them with me.

"I'm sure this won't be an easy day, but I hope that remembering how incredible he is will help a teeny bit," Morgan wrote.

She sent me stories I remembered and ones I didn't—silly and sentimental and everything in between. Morgan reminded me of the time we bought tickets to see *Dear Evan Hansen* at the Smith Center and my mom came with us.

"Your mom told us how your dad was pretty bummed out to not be the one taking us to the show," Morgan reminded me. "He probably couldn't have cared less about seeing the show, but he just wanted to be the one taking us! It was so funny then and now it seems even sweeter."

It was true; Dad despised musicals. But he suffered through so many of them just because I loved them and he wanted to spend time with me. What an incredible way to show his love.

"I know he's so happy to see you doing the things you're doing and being the person you are," Morgan wrote. "He is so lucky to have you, and you are so lucky to have him. He really is the best, and the reunion will be so sweet."

Morgan testified to me that Heavenly Father loves me.

"He and your dad are watching over you every day," she said. "Happy Father's Day!"

I finished reading and contemplating, and I looked out on a bright, brand-new Sunday. And my heart didn't feel so heavy anymore.

I was stepping gingerly through uncharted territory, an old holiday with brand-new significance. There were still moments that hurt, but there were even more moments that healed, especially with the day's mood set by Morgan's sweet letter.

Later in sacrament meeting, I looked up to see who was speaking at the pulpit and was met with a warm, familiar smile from my dear friend Reanna. Her words were mostly about Church history, about Nauvoo and Carthage and the faith of the early Saints. She talked about trials and faith, about God and joy, about all she'd learned from the beautiful Church history trip we'd gone on. It was Father's Day, but she wasn't speaking about fathers. I felt relieved, in a sense, that the day was being treated like any other.

We reached the end of her talk, however, and Reanna threw in a comment I wasn't expecting.

"On Father's Day," Reanna said, "we shouldn't just thank our earthly dads—we should remember to thank our Heavenly Father, too."

I had never before considered that Father's Day is not just about the dad who gave me his freckles and taught me how to drive—it is about the Father who gave me my very existence, the one who watches over and guides me every day.

A. Theodore Tuttle of the Seventy said it best: "It should have great meaning that of all the titles of respect and honor and admiration that could be given him, that God himself, he who is the highest of all, chose to be addressed simply as 'Father.'"[1]

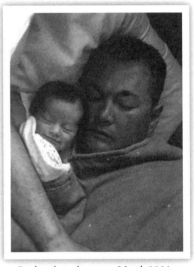

Dad and newborn me, March 2001.

What a sweet, sweet gift.

As I was floating through that afternoon with these gentle thoughts cradling my eggshell heart, I was hit by an unexpected impression: *What if I reached out to others who had lost their dads?*

"Happy Father's Day! Here's to our wonderful dads, to the legacy they've left us, and to the people they've shaped us

---

1. A. Theodore Tuttle, "The Role of Fathers," *Ensign*, January 1974.

to become," I texted a friend. "I love you. My heart is with you today."

I sent similar messages to several other friends and was touched by their responses. Connecting with others who shared common experiences helped me to emerge from my personal pity party and to instead remember how deeply the people around me were hurting. One responded, "I was sitting here feeling bad for myself, not even realizing that people I know are going through the same thing. We'll get through it together!"

Father's Day was stormy and had the potential to deepen my raw wounds. But despite that, and with the help of so many God-guided people around me, healing continued. Miracles took place. Light persisted, even in that darkness.

Regrowth

While we normally might have raked the leaves in our front yard together into small piles and then burned them, Mom took it upon herself in the fall of 2018 to set nearly the whole yard aflame instead.

We laughed for months over the charred mess that our yard had become. Everything was blackened, scorched. She was minorly sheepish but mostly unapologetic—at least the leaves were gone, she pointed out.

By summer 2019, I'd forgotten about the burning. Mid-June, however, as my mom and I stood at the kitchen sink washing dishes, she paused and looked out the window at the lawn.

"Look," she said suddenly, fascinated. "The grass is growing there in places it didn't before."

She pointed out areas that had been barren for as long as we'd lived there but now had tendrils of grass sprouting up, livening our yard.

I looked out across the lawn contemplatively. I thought of how our family had been burned. I thought of how we were growing in ways that we had never had to before.

"In a paradoxical way, afflictions and sorrow prepare us to experience joy if we will trust in the Lord and His plan for us," testified Elder L. Todd Budge.[1] He quoted the thirteenth-century poet Rumi, who said:

> Sorrow prepares you for joy. It violently sweeps everything out of your house, so that new joy can find space to enter. It shakes the yellow leaves from the bough of your heart, so that fresh, green leaves can grow in their place. It pulls up the rotten roots, so that new roots hidden beneath have room to grow. Whatever sorrow shakes from your heart, far better things will take their place.

There is beauty in the burning. There is purpose in the upheaval. We are learning to grow, you see. We are green tendrils unfurling towards the light.

We are not the fire that burned us. We are what we build out of the ashes. We are the brand-new growth that comes from the grief.

This is the hurting, and this is the healing, too.

We are becoming better than we ever were before.

---

1. L. Todd Budge, "Consistent and Resilient Trust," *Ensign*, November 2019.

Two Months

At our annual Independence Day gathering on Big Lake, I looked everywhere for Dad. I expected him to be chatting over the grill with my uncles, roasting perfect s'mores by the fire, or playing with my little brothers on the dock. But, of course, he was nowhere to be found. There was an unfamiliar kind of hollowness on this day that there hadn't been before.

Relatives casually brought up my dad in conversation. They mentioned concerts and heavy metal music. They talked about how fun it *was* to go crabbing with him on the ocean when we visited Washington in the summers. How helpful he *was*, how fun he *was*. About the world he colored and filled and left behind.

And finally the past-tense verbs they used became too grating on my ears and the feeling of missing him was too loud, hurting my heart, and I had to escape. I headed out to the quiet, empty dock on the lake. A sob ripped out of my throat.

I couldn't decide which was worse—the people who acted like he never existed, or the people who talked about him like he's gone for good. It still felt too fresh, too personal, too sacred to discuss. My sensitive heart took every word more personally than it was meant to.

"I want you here," I whispered to him across the rippling black waves.

It had only been two months. Exactly two months that day. I couldn't believe I'd made it that far, but even more than that, I could not fathom how far I still had to go. I was back at the north rim of the Grand Canyon looking out, overwhelmed, at the miles and miles left to go.

I watched bats flit over the glassy surface of Big Lake. Water splashed rhythmically against the floating dock, pulling it back and forth across the waves. Fireworks erupted in bright bursts, leaving reflective trails of red and gold sparks over the water.

When my heartbeat was calmed and my haggard breaths quieted by the soothing sound of the water, I returned to the party along the shore. Aunt Cindy sidled over to me, squeezed me in a hug, and looked up intently into my eyes.

"How have you done today?" she whispered. "Has it been okay?"

She was the first relative to comment on the significance of the date. She was the first one here to remember.

"It's weird," I confessed. "It's weird to be here, doing what we've always done, celebrating without him. But it would feel weird to be anywhere else instead, I guess."

"It's making new memories. Having new experiences," Cindy smiled. I thought of the game of KanJam we had laughed over earlier, the delicious fruit salad Mom and I had made and brought to share, the advice my cousins had given me about starting college. It was all the same—the same lake, the same Fourth of July traditions, the same relatives—but it was all brand new, too.

Cindy wrapped her arms around me and whispered, "I pray for you. Did you know that? Every day. And you know what I pray for?"

"What?" I asked, hugging her back.

"That you will be able to feel a little bit of peace, every day," she said. "At least one small moment, every single day."

We drifted back into the crowd of family members, and the conversation shifted to other subjects. But I lingered on the comfort that her words had provided. I looked out across the water and felt chills from head to toe, and not just from the damp evening. As I watched the glittery magic of red fireworks exploding across the lake, I thought, *This is not easy. But this is how it is supposed to be. And it is right.*

I watched my uncle hurry out to the dock in excitement, holding aloft a green paper lantern. He lit the base of the lantern and raised it overhead before letting it float into the darkness. The illuminated orb wobbled its way skyward, slowly but surely, until it was nothing but a glowing speck against the fading ashen sky.

Green. Bright green. And glowing.

I thought of my dad's radiant green eyes, the way they smile even when his mouth doesn't. They set his whole face aglow.

The idea of an eye being single to the glory of God popped into my mind.

"The light of the body is the eye: if therefore thine eye be single, thy whole body shall be full of light" (Matthew 6:22).

I can see the light, Dad, I smiled.

You are in it.

Paddleboarding

Growing up in the hot Mojave Desert without a swimming pool meant that bodies of water of any kind were largely foreign to me. Be it a rec center pool or the boundless ocean, I was afraid and uncertain of myself on water. I took a few years of swim lessons as a child and endured two anxiety-infused years on the high school swim team, but none of that abated my fear.

It was a warm summer day in Washington. I stood at the edge of Big Lake, twiddling my thumbs, pacing back and forth along the dock. Finally, I decided to feel the fear and take action anyway. I changed into my swimsuit and asked Aunt Cindy to come paddleboarding with me. My desire to learn a new skill—and my boredom—had finally overpowered my anxiety.

Cindy and I brushed off the dried algae and dead spiders and hoisted the boards onto our backs, making our way down the rocky shoreline. After tentatively navigating the tangled weeds growing along the edge of the lake, we pushed ourselves out onto the open water.

I rose shakily to my knees as Aunt Cindy and I paddled farther into the busy, rippling water. Boats raced by, rocking our boards back and forth.

ONE BREATH AT A TIME

"Are you going to try standing up?" Aunt Cindy asked as we paddled along on our knees.

"I don't know," I laughed. "I don't think I can do it."

I felt more secure when I was crouched, but I finally realized that I wasn't content to stay there. With Cindy's encouragement, I rose to my feet. I faced my toes outward, perpendicular to the board's nose, like I imagined I would do on a surfboard.

The board swayed beneath me, and I nearly toppled into the cold lake. I immediately crouched back down and gripped the edges of the board, settling my knees safely beneath me.

"Turn your feet parallel to the board this time," Cindy advised.

I waited until the nearest boat passed and the waters began to calm once more. Then, I rose again, this time with my feet in the proper position. My legs trembled as I tried to stabilize myself.

"You're doing it!" Cindy encouraged.

I beamed.

We paddled along the lake's shoreline, taking in the beauty of the doll-like houses, ridges of trees, and the foggy outline of Mount Baker in the distance.

A boat sped towards us, its motor roaring.

"There are big waves coming. Ride them out," Aunt Cindy said. "If you can withstand those, you can do anything."

She was referring to literal waves, but I couldn't help but make connections to the figurative paddleboard of grief I was riding as I paddled forward through the tumultuous water. Grieving was a brand-new experience for me, something I'd never done before, just as I had never before picked up a paddleboard. And just as my aunt was riding next to me, there are others on these same waters of grief, but they are standing on paddleboards of their own. Their experiences are solitary. Unique.

I realized there were still big waves of grief coming that I might not be expecting. I wouldn't be able to hold on the first time I tried. I might fall in a few times. But that was okay. If I could learn to withstand this current tumult, I would become tough enough to handle anything else that came my way. If I'd already survived two months of this, I could survive two months more. And who knew what I could accomplish after that?

I didn't expect to paddleboard perfectly the first time I tried, I thought. *So why did I expect myself to know how to grieve perfectly when I had never done this before?*

I am riding it out. Sometimes I lose my footing. But always, always, there is a way to keep going. Eventually, these waves will not be able to crash over me anymore.

Peter on the Water

In Matthew 14, Peter and the other Apostles are resting in their boat when the Savior walks to them across the stormy sea. In his excitement, Peter asks Christ if he can join Him in walking on the water.

With Christ's encouragement, and focusing on His countenance, Peter steps out of the boat and begins to walk across the surface of the sea. As the storm grows more violent, however, he loses sight of the Savior and instead focuses on the fierce winds and tumultuous waves.

"Lord," Peter cries in fear as he begins to sink. "Save me!"

As Christ reaches forward to catch Peter, He says, "O thou of little faith, wherefore didst thou doubt?" (v. 31).

I love to think of that encounter as a hugely faith-defining moment for Peter. When Peter kept his focus on his Savior, he did not falter; it was only when he came to fear the waves more than he loved the Lord that he faltered.

Most of all, I hope Peter learned that Christ, in His mercy, was there waiting to catch Peter the entire time he was walking across the water. He never left him alone.

He fell, but he was lifted, and soon he would have the chance to act as the Savior had in lifting another fallen soul. In Acts 3, as Peter and John walk up to the temple, a disabled man resting on the steps of the building asks the Apostles for alms. This man has spent years sitting here in front of the temple. All he expects is to receive a little money and to have to return the next day for more. This is his life.

But Peter has something more to give him. Something unexpected. Something miraculous.

"Look on us," Peter commands the man. "Silver and gold have I none; but such as I have give I thee: In the name of Jesus Christ of Nazareth rise up and walk" (vv. 4, 6).

It is then that the most glorious parallel takes place. Just as Christ lifted Peter at a time when he could not stand, Peter "took [the disabled man] by the right hand, and lifted him up: and immediately his feet and ankle bones received strength" (v. 7).

Peter had been unable to walk spiritually. This disabled man had never stood on his feet. But now he arose and went into the temple, "walking, and leaping, and praising God" (v. 8).

I like to think that as Peter lifted that man and changed his life, as he beheld the immense rapture he'd brought him, that perhaps he thought back to the time when he, too, had been unable to stand.

I like to think he thought of the Savior lifting him up.

Just as Peter began to sink as he walked across the choppy waves, it is easy to be swept away in the sea of grief. It is easy to think, "There is no one who has ever felt this way. There is no one who knows my pain. There is no way I can get through this."

But just as Peter looked to our Savior for help and was later able to help another to rise, there are many around us who have been through the waters of grief before and who can help guide us to safety. Along with our Savior, who knows

ONE BREATH AT A TIME

our pains perfectly because of His suffering in the Garden of Gethsemane, there are countless living angels around us who know what it is like to be on a solitary paddleboard in the rocky waters of sorrow. By leaning on each other and offering each other our support, we can grow to be more like Peter, and ultimately more like our Savior. We can rise from the sea of grief and lift others who are losing their footing.

One of my Peters is my Aunt Ali, my dad's sister-in-law. Just like me, she was a senior in high school when her father died. The night after I lost my dad, when I was unsure where to turn for guidance and comfort, I reached out to her.

"How do you get through this?" I texted her in anguish. "How did you do this?"

What followed was a much-needed dose of realism, empathy, and love.

"I wish I could say something that would help, but nothing helps," she responded just a few minutes later. "You have to take one day at a time, one hour at a time, one minute at a time. And some days you'll do okay, and other days are just going to plain suck!"

Even though that message seemed scary at first, it was reassuring, too; it validated the pain I was experiencing. Grieving was going to take time, and I was allowed to take that time. I was allowed to feel sorrow, to walk in that darkness, and to know I did not walk in it alone. I was allowed to take it one breath at a time.

"Remember the good times," Aunt Ali advised. She told me it might take a while to be able to talk about Dad with my family again and that it was difficult for her at first.

"It made everyone so sad, and I hated being sad. It was my

job to make everyone happy," she said. "I was the fixer. I see a lot of that in you. And the really hard part is you can't fix this one."

Oh, it's true, I thought, and the reality of the situation hit me like a gut-punch once again. *I can't fix this one.*

"And you're going to get angry and wonder why. But please don't let this change your path. You are so amazing and have such an amazing future ahead of you. Don't let this define you. Don't have a chip on your shoulder and think, 'Poor me,'" Aunt Ali advised. She added that I needed to go to school, to go experience new parts of life, to stay busy.

It was an important reminder, one I would repeat to myself for months to come.

It's allowed to hurt, and it does, I would tell myself. *But I don't get to pity myself. I get to choose to heal. I get to choose to keep going.*

"Heavenly Father needs the good ones," she told me.

It was those final words that filled me with the most hope of all.

If Heavenly Father needs the good ones, I thought with resolve, *I'm going to be so good. I'm going to be the best I can be.*

It was reassuring to hear my aunt's advice and to know that she had survived the same thing I was now going through. Like Peter, Ali was lifted from the waters of sorrow, and she, in turn, helped to lift me from a trial I did not know how to bear on my own.

I found my next Peter in early June. As I traveled across the American Midwest with my fellow high school graduates on our Church-history trip, I met Beckee, an adviser for the trip who had lost her dad when she was just fourteen. I found

ONE BREATH AT A TIME

unparalleled strength in her wit and wisdom. Still drowning in the sea of grief and looking for direction, I latched onto Beckee's lifeboat and have not let go since.

One night when I was struggling to wade through my grief alone, Heavenly Father sent Beckee my way. I had not reached out to her and had not asked for her help, but she already knew exactly what I needed to hear.

"My dear—I don't know if you need to know this today or not, but please know that Heavenly Father and your earthly father love you so much and are aware of you," she texted me.

I was flooded with love. I began sending her my pressing questions about how to move on, how to heal, and how to live with pain. Beckee responded with great empathy.

"It's not easy to try to figure out how to keep going on. Especially when you want the past back, but the future keeps coming," Beckee texted. "I remember thinking so many times right after my dad's death, 'Does this actually even matter?' And just feeling pain like I never knew could exist."

It's not just me, I thought. *I'm not alone in this.*

Beckee offered counsel as well, showing me deeper insights into the meaning behind my pain and regrets. She said, "I feel like a couple things could be happening right now. . . . I feel as though you are growing in a way in which the adversary is very displeased. You are deepening your ability to keep your present covenants and more fully embrace your future ones."

I hadn't thought of it like that. It made me feel stronger to know that if I was struggling, it was not only because of my grief—it was because I was at war with Satan, and I was winning by continuing to progress. I was not letting the waves of grief sweep me away.

"I didn't realize at fourteen (and still don't truly to this day) just how much pain is a refiner and connector to Christ," Beckee said.

I told her how afraid I was that I would never get through my pain, my brain-fogged confusion, my depression. What if this pain never ended?

"How do you do it?" I asked. "How do you press play when your brain is still stuck in rewind?"

"This will pass, this anxiety, this concern, this brain-stuckedness. It truly will," she reassured me. "Satan . . . wants you to believe that this is how it is. Period. Or maybe even that this is who *you* are. Period. . . . He is very bitter and seeks to tell us lies."

It struck me how true her words were. I *did* believe that my life would always be this way. I was so stuck in my own pain that I could see no farther than a few feet ahead of me in the darkness. I was swimming in shallow waters, but because I could not see the floor, the ocean felt bottomless.

"You can call upon the powers of heaven more fervently, knowing that perhaps it isn't quite time for you to be out of this experience. But just as we learned with Joseph [Smith], 'All these things shall give thee experience, and shall be for thy good,'" said Beckee (D&C 122:7).

It isn't quite time for me to be freed from this. I have more to learn. God has more to teach me. I will be patient in waiting, in learning, in growing.

"I know that you will have great moments of peace even if the only thing that changes is internal," Beckee promised. "You will feel that sound mind more fully someday soon.

ONE BREATH AT A TIME

Remember, faith in God includes faith in God's timing.[1] He knows who you are, where you are, and the great desires of your heart. Be present with Him."

Be present with Him. Turn to Him. Give this to Him.

Nothing was getting better in my life, but *I* was getting better. And I knew it was because of Him.

As I read through Beckee's powerful words and comforting insights, I was reminded again of Peter. Just as he showed us with his experiences on the ocean and at the temple, we learn how to uplift others as we go through our own times of being too weak to stand. We learn to paddle through the waters of grief so that we can teach the next newcomer how to stay afloat. Just as Aunt Ali and Beckee lifted me with their stories and insights and love, I aim to become a Peter for someone else, to lift someone else to their feet.

It is not easy. We do not always say the right things. And we will never truly know how another person feels, for every circumstance is unique.

But as we call upon God to give us empathy and courage, He will mold us and guide us in ways that will allow us to be instruments in His hands. He will teach us, just as Christ taught Peter, how to lift others who have fallen. How to see the good in our trials. How to rise, like the man at the temple, "walking, and leaping, and praising God."

We are not alone. There are hands reaching out all around us to raise us up.

"I am here, I am here, I am here."

We will not swim in the sea of sorrow forever.

---

1. See Neal A. Maxwell, "Lest Ye Be Wearied and Faint in Your Minds," *Ensign*, May 1991.

Bitter

As I look back through old notes and journal entries from the first few months of my grief, I am struck by how bitter and angry I was in the immediate aftermath of my father's death. Try as I might have to keep myself from growing negative and dark, I still felt a hard shell developing over me. It was a defense mechanism in response to how hurt and vulnerable I felt.

It was the end of my senior year of high school, and my peers were discussing how much they were going to miss their friends as they left to serve Church missions. All I could think was, *That's only two years, guys. I'm not going to see my dad again in this life. You have no idea what "missing" feels like. You have no idea what it means to mourn.*

It was not a logical comparison, but I still felt angry and hurt. The distance I felt from them grew greater and greater each day as I stewed beneath my storm cloud.

I found a note from around the time of graduation that read, "I do not want to be angry. My soft, still heart is aching. I do not want that heart to burst. But sometimes that sadness becomes irritability and anger. Sometimes it's not enough to know how well you mean. You sympathize with me but cannot empathize. Even if you have been in the throng of grief, you do not know mine. You try. I know you try. But you do not know. And at the end of the day, you go home and hug your dad and breathe a sigh of relief that it isn't you, that you haven't lost yours. I don't get to go home from that."

I wasn't angry at God, and I wasn't really angry at anybody in particular. I just remember feeling so deeply hurt that I was bitter towards everyone. Nobody could possibly know how badly I was hurting. Nobody could take that away from me.

That summer, I wrote, "Here's the part of the grief that no one tells you about: It's the anger at nothing and no one and everything and everyone. I just want Dad here. Then I'd be less irritable. I'm sorry that I am letting my hurt make me bitter. I will be bitter until I can grow into something better. I am trying. I swear, I am trying."

I thought I would feel that way forever.

I thought this was who I had to be now, that I was stuck, forever, in the spiral of grief and anger and isolation.

But I think you have to let yourself be bitter for a little while so that you can turn sweet again. I think you have to become familiar with that pain to know the peace of relief once more. I think our joy is relative to our experiences, that the caverns of our misery give greater contrast to our mountains of elation.

I think it hurts before it heals.

A famous refrain teaches, "If you are going through hell, keep going." We cannot bypass the struggle. The only way out is through.

I froze and hardened that summer. But gradually the ice melted. Little by little, that hard shell cracked. I began to learn that every pain is valid and unique. Your pain is valid if you miss your missionaries. Your grief is valid, whether it is your dad or your dog or a public figure that you've lost. Your pain is valid if your loved one suffered from illness for many months before passing away and you agonized by their bedside, and it is valid if they died unexpectedly without giving you the chance to say goodbye. We all experience a variety of pain and sorrow and loss. There is no way to quantify our grief. There is no way to equalize what we have lost.

The only thing that matters, then, is that all our pains, big and small, are "swallowed up in the joy of Christ" (Alma 31:38). It is in Him that the bitter turns sweet again. It is in Him that we trade our sorrow for joy.

Would I Ever Do Anything to Hurt You?

I am twelve years old, standing in my parents' bathroom while my dad shaves his face. He pulls me over to the sink with him and, teasing, brings the still-whirring razor to my cheek. I recoil, afraid.

"It tickles!" he laughs. "It doesn't hurt."

Still, I shake my head.

"Gabrielle," he says, looking me directly, almost sternly, in the eye. "Would I ever do anything to hurt you?"

The night my dad died, I prayed so fervently for him to be healed. Even as the paramedics knelt on the floor around my father, trying to bring him back to life, even as the minutes ticked by to no avail, I was filled with unshakable, impenetrable faith. I knew, with utmost certainty, that Dad would make it out alive. I knew that God would let us keep him.

But then he died. I had never seen it coming, could never imagine a reality without him in it. I was crushed. I lay there on the floor beside him, in his blood and my tears.

Yet I felt, even then, an unshakable love for my Heavenly Father.

"I love you," I prayed. "And I know you love us. But I do not understand."

I wrestled for months on end with the juxtaposition of

believing in a loving God and yet feeling that He had forsaken me. Why was it that my prayers—my righteous desires—were not answered the way I wanted them to be?

Everywhere I went, I felt like I was bombarded with reminders of how God had forsaken my family. Old women bore their testimonies in sacrament meetings of how God was watching out for them. Seminary students shared experiences of prayers that were answered—lost earrings that were recovered, anxieties that were soothed, cars that started.

Dad on a family vacation in Puerto Rico, August 2013.

Why is God watching out for them and not for me? Did I not pray fervently enough? Isn't He listening to my prayers? What did I do wrong?

But I knew there had to be a lesson. I knew there had to be some reason behind it, or this was not the God I knew. He was watching out for me in that He knew I had something I needed to learn. I did pray fervently, and it reminded me how much I value communing with God. He was listening to my prayers, and He did answer them, but the answer was, "No—I have something else in mind. I'm looking out for you."

President Spencer W. Kimball taught, "If all the sick for whom we pray were healed, if all the righteous were protected and the wicked destroyed, the whole program of the Father would be annulled and the basic principle of the gospel, free agency, would be annulled. No man would have to live by faith."[1]

Faith is not about having all of our desires met exactly as we ask for them. We do not know the meaning of trust, I think, until God breaks through our preference and shows us that He has something better in mind.

I found further comfort in 1 Nephi 11:17, where I learned that not even faithful Nephi had all the answers.

"I know that he loveth his children," said Nephi of our Heavenly Father. "Nevertheless, I do not know the meaning of all things."

We are learning truth and meaning, little by little, through every trial and faith-building experience. It does not come at once. We say, "I do not understand, dear Father," and He says, "Let me show you. Let me teach you."

I am learning as I am healing to let God be who He is without trying to change His will or redirect His plan. To say, "Not my will, but thine be done."

Make my will as yours.
Here is my hand. Please take it.
Please show me the way.

Even as I lay there in the initial exhaustion and ache, even as the pain hit again and again, I realized that it was going to be okay. My suffering has purpose. I am growing, even now, even here.

Because of our Savior's sacrifice, our pain has purpose.

---

1. *Teachings of Presidents of the Church: Spencer W. Kimball* (2006), 15.

Our trials can ennoble us, our spirits can be refined, and we can make diamonds out of coal.

We have to go through the refining fire in this life, whether we want to or not. But when we lean on God, trusting in Christ's Atonement, trusting in His timing, trusting that His ways are higher than our ways—

It is then that we find purpose in our pain.

It is then that Christ teaches us what true joy looks like.

We appreciate food more after fasting, for our hunger gives context and power to the delicious satisfaction available to our tastebuds. We enjoy peaceful Sundays after an exhausting work week and take joy in stretching and resting after a hard workout. It is the contrast of struggling, persevering, and working that refines us. We are Joseph Smith in the Sacred Grove all over again, blinded by God's brilliance after being smothered by Satan's darkness. It is the deepest sorrow that paves the way for the greatest joy.

I still don't fully understand why my dad doesn't get to be here with us anymore. It breaks my heart. But I know, too, that just like my dad standing there with a razor in his hand, my Heavenly Father is not trying to hurt me.

He is giving me experiences. Teaching me. Molding me.

"For a small moment have I forsaken thee, but with great mercies will I gather thee" (3 Nephi 22:7).

"Would I ever do anything to hurt you?" He asks. "Would I ever let something happen if it weren't going to change your life for the better, if it weren't going to mold you into the person you need to become?"

No, Heavenly Father. You wouldn't.

Changes

I don't want my grief to harden me.
I do not want to let this burden turn me
Into something I wasn't
Before.

But there is beauty, too
In this vulnerability.

I am hurting, I say.
I am healing, too.

And maybe I change.
Maybe now,
I have to.

But maybe I get to choose the change.
Maybe this softens me.
Maybe now my heart
Won't be quite
So hard.

Maybe the soft heart
Is the one that heals itself
And others.

Maybe this changes me
For good.

GABRIELLE SHIOZAWA

How many kind people
Have told me I'm wonderful—
"Don't ever change!"
How trite; I hope
I hope
I hope I change.

I hope there's something better
That God can shape
Out of me.

What They Don't Tell You

Here's what they don't tell you about grief:
It doesn't get easier. You don't stop missing them. It doesn't get better.
But here's what does happen:
YOU get better.
If you let it, this can become the most spiritually sanctifying time of your life. You will be in immense pain, but you can also know immense peace. The two can coexist.

"Therefore if any man be in Christ, he is a new creature: old things are passed away; behold, all things are become new" (2 Corinthians 5:17).

You are a new creature.

You are experiencing a minute facet of what our Savior suffered through.

You think that you have been buried, but instead, you've been planted.

And, my dear friend, you are going to bloom.

BYU: Completely, Utterly, at Home

Written for the George H. Brimhall
Memorial Essay Contest at BYU, Fall 2019

One does not normally face the glassy-eyed, overeager expression of Chuck E. Cheese with a smile. Yet the photographic evidence is unmistakable. My dad holds my one-year-old self aloft, anticipating my reaction, as I come nose-to-nose with Chuck. But the expression on my toddler face is neither fear nor hesitation—it is complete and utter delight.

I have always loved mascots. In every opportunity to meet a larger-than-life hero, there was one constant: my dad. He always stood in line with me, ushered me forward, and snapped a picture as I hugged my idols. And the excitement didn't end there; with Chuck E. Cheese came pizza and prizes. Meeting the Mariner Moose meant the thrill of sharing nachos and a baseball game with Dad. It was never just about the mascots; it was about the joy and connection they represented.

Yet I had not considered mascots in quite some time when a new face arrived in the mail: Cosmo's smiling visage on a 4" x 4" magnet.

"Cosmo was created to represent and further the 'Spirit of the Y,'" wrote *Daily Universe* reporter Judy Lambert in

ONE BREATH AT A TIME

1962. "He accomplishes this by being a living symbol of which the school can be proud."

I pondered what BYU meant to me. Three grandparents studied here, and my parents met on this campus. Was I to continue that legacy?

I looked at Cosmo—the Spirit of the Y—and knew, even before I'd set foot on these grounds, that BYU had the potential to feel just like home.

Dad and me meeting Chuck E. Cheese, September 2002.

So, with Cosmo cheering me on from the fridge, I submitted my application and began preparing for life as a Cougar. Once I was accepted, I began fantasizing about moving in. Dad would drive me to school, offer me his sage advice, and take me to find Cosmo. I would finally hug the mascot who had made this all possible.

Everything was on track.

Then, three weeks before my high school graduation, Dad collapsed on our living room floor. Instead of writing my valedictorian address, I wrote a eulogy for my dad's funeral. Instead of looking forward to a future of exciting opportunities at BYU, I wondered how I could endure the next year, let alone the next five minutes, without my dad.

When the time came, I drove myself to Provo. I quietly unpacked my boxes. Although I looked for him everywhere, Cosmo was nowhere to be found.

I was finally a Cougar, but I did not want to rise and shout. I wanted to sit down and cry. I felt completely, utterly alone.

As classes began, and as I settled into college life, I carefully took note of each student I passed. Even though I could not find Cosmo anywhere on campus, I beheld his spirit in every one of my peers.

"BYU is a very international, cosmopolitan school," commented Daniel T. Gallego, who was the first to don the Cosmo costume in October 1953. "That is where we got the name Cosmo."[1]

Some of my peers crossed oceans to come to BYU. Some made great sacrifices to be here. Every one of us brought heavy burdens with us as we stepped foot into the unknown.

Beyond the heartache of my peers, however, I have found something greater. I see kindness and fervor. I see passion and drive. I see an entire university full of people with ambitions and hopes so ardent they make them want to rise and shout.

Finally, game day arrives, and I join my peers for my first-ever BYU football game. As I take my place in the stands, enraptured by the energy of the crowd, I look out onto the field. What I see causes a familiar tremble to rise in my heart.

What I see is Cosmo.

Standing in the middle of the field.

With his fist raised high in the air.

---

1. "Cosmo," byucougars.com; https://byucougars.com/page/cosmo. Accessed February 2021.

ONE BREATH AT A TIME

That rush comes over me again—my dad standing in line with me, nudging me forward to chase my dreams, waiting for me with a smile on his face. That sheer thrill, a thousand times over, of feeling loved and hopeful and completely, utterly, at home.

BYU scores. My peers rise to their feet. I am lost in the roar.

Triumphant, I rise and shout.

⌄⌃

While many expressed excitement after hearing about my second-place victory in this essay contest, few asked what I had written about.

But my friend Barbara did. When she posed the question, I hesitated, wondering just how to describe the pain that I had poured into this essay. Finally, instead of trying to explain it, I handed her the paper to read for herself.

I waited in anticipation and watched my friend's eyes grow watery as she scanned through my writing.

At last she looked up, and I braced myself for a typical response, an "I'm so sorry" or "I can't even imagine" or something else that everybody says.

But instead, she looked up at me, her eyes full of tears behind her bangs and glasses. Barbara smiled and whispered, "I don't know him, but I feel like I do, because I know you."

It struck me then that the reason others can know my dad through knowing me, the reason my dad's life shines in my countenance, is because I remember him always. He impacts every action I take and every word I say.

I finally understand what the sacrament prayers mean

when they say that we "are willing to take upon them the name of thy Son, and always remember him" (Moroni 4:3). I get how we "do always remember him, that they may have his Spirit to be with them" (Moroni 5:2). I always wondered why it was so important to "always remember him" that it was mentioned twice. But now I get it:

What if remembering my dad always and having his countenance shine through me teaches me how to remember my Savior better?

What if we can learn to remember our Savior in all things so perfectly that people who have never known Him will know Him through us?

Barbara looks up at me again.

"Tell me about him," she says.

Stories of Dad

Dad is always telling stories, and he watches the same movies on repeat if he loves the message enough. I've always thought it was silly of him, but more and more lately I am unearthing connections between the stories Dad loves and the philosophies he uses in life.

"One way to remember who you are is to remember who your heroes are," Dad wrote in a notebook he left behind. I believe this is why he loves stories so much; because it helps him find examples of people he wants to emulate. Dad does not just passively observe a story; he jumps into it, interacts with it, and comes out with lasting lessons and changed actions.

Dad references on repeat a story Brother Randall L. Ridd told in a 2015 devotional at BYU–Idaho called "The Parable of the Oranges." In the parable, Brother Ridd illustrated the principle of living with real intent by telling the story of a young man at a company who was upset his coworker had received a promotion when he had not. To answer the man's complaints, his boss issued a challenge to him to go to the grocery store and buy some oranges for the boss's wife.

"What kind of oranges did you buy?" the boss asked when the man returned.

"I don't know. You just said to buy oranges, and these are oranges. Here they are," said the man.

The boss then asked him to stay and watch while he issued the same challenge to the man who had just received a promotion. He was asked the same question by the boss when he returned, but he gave a vastly different response.

"Well, the store had many varieties—there were navel oranges, Valencia oranges, blood oranges, tangerines, and many others, and I didn't know which kind to buy," the man explained. "But I remembered you said your wife needed the oranges, so I called her. She said she was having a party and that she was going to make orange juice."

The man went on to explain that he consulted the grocer to see which oranges made the best orange juice, asked him how many he needed to buy, and even convinced the grocer to give him a quantity discount.

Brother Ridd pointed out in this parable that the difference between the two young men was their intentions.

"You might say that one went the extra mile, or one was more efficient, or one paid more attention to detail, but the most important difference had to do with real intent rather than just going through the motions," Brother Ridd taught. "The first young man was motivated by money, position, and prestige. The second young man was driven by an intense desire to please his employer and an inner commitment to be the best employee he could possibly be—and the outcome was obvious."[1]

I never used to understand why Dad loved "The Parable

---

1. Randall L. Ridd, "Living with Purpose: The Importance of 'Real Intent,'" Worldwide Devotional for Young Adults, January 11, 2015.

of the Oranges" so much, but it is clear to me now that this lesson left an indelible impression on him because it showed him a more Christlike way to serve. He consistently applied that lesson in his everyday life.

It was April 2019, and Dad had just come home from Vegas with a back seat full of Costco goodies.

"Here, Boo," Dad beamed, handing me a Neapolitan-flavored snack mix. "I thought this would be fun for your party this weekend."

I was planning on having a few people over that weekend to make cookies and stargaze together. I had only mentioned my plans casually and had not asked Dad for anything special, yet of his own volition he had gone out of his way to find something new and fun for my friends and me to enjoy.

This is how he has always been. I have distinct memories of being invited to birthday parties in elementary school and having Dad excitedly jump in to see what gift I wanted to bring. I once mentioned it would be fun to buy some different colors of nail polish for a friend. When he came home that day, not only did he have a dozen different colors for me to choose from, but he had picked out some nail files, nail polish remover, and a few different kinds of nail pens and stickers I'd never seen before.

"This way, you can put together lots of fun things for your friend," Dad grinned. With a wink, he added, "Plus, I got extra so that you could keep some, too."

My dad could have acted like the young man in "The Parable of the Oranges" who obediently bought some oranges without much thought. He could have just grabbed the first nail polish he saw and thrown it in the cart. But instead, he put his heart into it. He used real intent. He wasn't "too manly" or "too busy" to pore over the nail polish selection and ask store clerks for their opinions. My dad acted like the man who had called the boss's wife and consulted the grocer to make sure he was making the best choice, and he went above and beyond to serve.

Dad also loved the 2015 Church video "Reach Out with Love," which taught the important lesson of reaching out to individuals with genuine love. He showed it often in Sunday School lessons, Bishop's Youth Council meetings, and family home evening because he loved how it illustrated what it meant to focus on seeing people as more than just a number and genuinely making friends with the people we fellowship. From making personal visits to check on people to dedicating his time to finding solutions for people in his stewardship, Dad used the philosophy of this video every day in his work in the Church.

Dad loved to find stories worth telling in everything. I hope he knows now that his life is exactly that kind of story.

I Ache for All We Did Not Do

The greatest pain involved in Dad's death, besides missing him, is having to live with regrets. There are so many times I took his goodness for granted. There were times we disagreed that we never resolved. There were so many ways he sacrificed for me to show me his love, and I didn't do enough to reciprocate.

Beyond regretting my actions, I mourn for the activities we never got to do together. There was a Hello Kitty Cafe that popped up in Las Vegas two months after he was gone—he would have made that so fun. The new Las Vegas Aviators' stadium opened up that season, but we didn't make time to get tickets before he was gone; we were planning on going later that May. There were so many baseball games we didn't get to go to. Nachos and ice cream and the best seats and the best baseball commentary with Dad. I read that there were all kinds of macaroni and cheese at the new stadium and a special apple pie à la mode in a baseball helmet, but if I try those someday it will have to be with someone else.

We went to a craft store once and looked at tiny plates and utensils at Dad's request. He excitedly described the party we could host, the tiny hors d'oeuvres we could make and all the fun ways we could decorate. He was constantly sending me food tutorial videos on Instagram for a variety of unique entrees and desserts.

"We need to try this one!" he'd say. But we never made time to try any of them. (You always think you have more time than you do.)

I had on my to-do list the instruction to record the sound of my parents' laughter. But I put it off again and again, instead pursuing more "important" things. But now I can hardly remember what his laugh sounded like.

I ache for all we did not do, Dad.

But I am still healed by all we did.

Troys

Early in my first semester of college, my roommate Jocelyn and I walked around campus, talking and getting to know each other. We laughed at stories about each other's families.

"And my dad, well," Jocelyn laughed. "I have the funniest story about how he met my mom."

"What's your dad's name?" I asked.

"Troy," she smiled.

My heart jumped into my throat.

"Troy?" I said. "That's *my* dad's name!"

"I guess our grandmas were both good at picking out names," Jocelyn laughed. "We'll have to have them meet up at some point! Your dad sounds like he'd be good friends with mine."

"Yeah!" I swallowed. I hadn't had the courage to tell my roommates about my dad's death just yet. "That would be so fun."

I met Jocelyn's Troy sooner than I'd expected when he came to town on a business trip and asked to take all the roommates to breakfast. We chatted and laughed over pancakes and French toast. As I watched Jocelyn and her dad interact with each other, jostling and joking, it reminded me a lot of my relationship with my father. I missed our inside jokes, his goofiness, his advice.

Our dads would get along so well, I mused. *They're both so fun and loving. They're both so crazy about their daughters . . .*

I had a twinge of pain, too, as I realized that I'd never get to introduce my dad to my roommates. He'd think Jocelyn and her dad were so fun.

It wasn't until Jocelyn's dad dropped us off again on campus and we headed back towards our apartment building that I realized what had really happened.

Celebrating Father's Day at a sushi restaurant, June 2018.

Dad was with us all along. Of course. He was eating pancakes with us and joking with us. He and the other Troy got along perfectly and bonded over families, work, and movie quotes. He met Jocelyn and shook his head at me, teasing me that I'd have to watch out, but secretly grateful that I had such a fun-loving roommate to get me out of my shell. I marveled at how easily I could picture him there, at how vividly I'd felt his spirit there with me.

"Isn't my dad the best?" Jocelyn beamed. "I love my dad! I can't wait for our dads to meet."

"I can't either," I smiled. "They'll love each other."

ONE BREATH AT A TIME

Later, after I'd finally confided in roommates about my loss, Jocelyn pulled me aside.

"Was it weird to go to breakfast with my dad?" she frowned. "I'm sorry for talking about my father so much."

I thought for a moment.

"No, not at all," I smiled. "It was perfect. It reminded me of being with my dad."

And there, right there, I felt at home.

Temples

I loved temples even before I lost my dad. Yet these sacred buildings, the peace I felt within them, and the promised blessings they provide hold even greater meaning for me now that he is gone.

In the first few days after Dad's death, stumbling through the tumult of grief, I knew only one thing for sure: I needed to be as close to the Spirit as possible.

That first Sunday, I took the sacrament as my friends wiped away my tears.

On Monday, I went to seminary—but not school.

And on Tuesday, when my father had been gone for only four days, when I hadn't the slightest idea how to keep living, I knew one decision I could make with absolute, perfect clarity: I needed to go to the temple.

Reanna skipped school with me, and we drove into Las Vegas to perform proxy baptisms. Because it was a weekday around noon, when everyone else was in school or at work, the baptistry was nearly empty. It was still, peaceful, and otherworldly—it was just what I needed.

Reanna and I worked our way through a stack of our ancestors' names. There was an incredible sense of peace and

ONE BREATH AT A TIME

purpose that came from being there in the Lord's house, performing ordinance work for our relatives.

After being baptized, we went to the confirmation room. During my confirmations, as my wet hair dripped down my back, the temple worker whose hands were on my head suddenly stopped speaking and lifted his hands from my head.

"Are these family names?" he whispered to me, looking around in wide-eyed wonder.

"Yes," I answered as I turned around to look at him. "Yes, they are."

He looked at me with awe.

"They're here," he murmured. "They're right here with us."

I looked around in silent wonder, as if my ancestors would start appearing before my eyes. The whole room felt unusually still. Peaceful. Joyous.

Reanna and I took our time leaving the temple that day. As we walked out into the warm Las Vegas sunlight, I pondered the connections I was making with my ancestors as I performed ordinance work for them. I thought back to the first time I'd ever performed temple baptisms.

It was February 16, 2013. I had turned twelve just six days earlier and was finally old enough to enter the temple. In honor of my grandpa's birthday that weekend, we planned a temple trip to the Seattle Washington Temple with many of my cousins, aunts, and uncles.

I was giddy. My shoulder blades arched and my chin stuck high in the air, I proudly handed over my brand-new temple recommend and went to get dressed in my clean white jumpsuit. I sat on a pew with my hands clasped excitedly, my legs swinging back and forth in thrill as I waited for my turn.

Finally, I joined my dad in the font, and he baptized me for Great-Grandma Gladys. I was overcome with elation. I can still picture the way my dad beamed at me as he extended his hand to me when I entered the water. It was one of the happiest days of my life.

More than six years passed between the first time I stepped foot in the Seattle temple and the second time, and this time it had brand-new significance. On our annual family trip to see relatives in Washington in July 2019, Mom and I made an outing to the Seattle temple to perform baptisms. Just the two of us.

It was even more beautiful than I had remembered. As I looked around the baptistry in awe, I pictured my twelve-year-old self bouncing on the pew. I remembered seeing my dad in the water, reaching out his hand, a smile on his face.

It felt like coming home.

Two months later during my first semester at BYU, I picked a Friday afternoon to go to the temple to perform baptisms. I had been at school for over two weeks without attending the temple—even though there were two in close proximity to me—and I was ready to feel an outpouring of the Spirit again as I knew I would find in the Lord's house.

The afternoon I chose arrived with an unexpected storm. Intense wind and pouring rain whipped my dress around my legs as I headed out the door and began walking up the street to the temple. I considered turning back as the wind turned my umbrella inside out and the rain soaked through my dress. *No*, I told myself fiercely. *Rain or shine, I committed to this.*

I was planning on walking to my car, which was parked across from the MTC, and driving it downtown to the beautiful Provo City Center Temple. On my way to the parking lot, however, I ran into three fellow freshmen who were all walking to the Provo temple up the street together. Just as I was about to part ways with them and head into the parking lot, a prompting hit me.

"Actually, I haven't been to this temple either," I said. "Can I just come with you guys?"

"Absolutely!" they beamed.

Our band of four marched through the rain together, and, even though we were soaked through by the time we got there, we were ultimately successful in reaching the temple. As we walked through the front doors, shaking out our umbrellas and wringing out our hair, I began to look around me. I realized that the Provo temple's layout appeared to be—at least from the entryway—almost exactly like that of the Seattle temple.

As I walked downstairs and took in the sight of the baptistry, I marveled at the similarities. From the stairway to the layout of the font to the design of the pews, I was reminded distinctly of that temple where I had performed baptisms for the very first time over six years earlier.

I sat there on the pew in my jumpsuit, and I felt more peace than I'd known in months come rushing over me.

Why has it taken you so long to go to the temple? I asked myself. *Why did you stay away?*

The Spirit responded, *So you would know, even more, how good it feels and how important it is to be here. So you could feel the difference.*

So you could find God here.

So you could find Dad here.

Finally, it hit me: Dad had been the one to send me that

prompting to come to this temple. He knew I'd find him here. He knew that in my tumultuous first weeks of school, when everything else around me seemed to be falling apart, I could go to this temple and remember why it was all worth it. I'd remember getting baptized for my great-grandma. I'd remember my dad, reaching out his hand. I'd remember where it all began.

I am overjoyed by our gospel, by our beautiful temples, by the goodness of our God.

In every darkness, you see, there is always this light.

You Know Me So Much Better Now

It was October during my first semester at BYU. As I was looking for a place to study on campus, I ran into Amber, a friend I had met while she was serving her mission in my hometown.

Amber told me she'd heard about my dad and how sorry she was. But beyond condolences, Amber went on to tell me the beautiful things she remembered, like how the sacrament meetings he conducted as bishop were the most spiritual meetings she's ever attended. She reminded me of a fast Sunday when he asked us to focus our testimonies on our gratitude for the Atonement over any other topic. Amber reminded me of the way the Spirit flooded the chapel that day.

"He always wore cowboy boots with his suit—even to the temple!" Amber laughed. I'd forgotten about that; I was so used to it that I considered it commonplace. She reminded me how special my dad is to everyone who knew him, how many people still love and admire and miss him. How widespread his reach truly is, this ripple effect spreading everywhere I go.

Amber pointed out a perspective I hadn't heard before: She talked about how she can sometimes feel her deceased grandmother's presence with her and that she feels that her grandma knows her better now than she ever did during mortality.

"It's hard not to have them here, but I think our loved ones know us even better now from the other side," she said gently. "I think we carry them with us differently. Do you feel that way?"

I thought of the wide range of experiences I'd had since my dad passed away—the quiet moments when I felt him with me, the times his advice and counsel came to mind when I needed it most. I remembered the time he nudged me to go talk to the bishop about my struggles and the peace that had come with that visit, the time when he prompted me to go to the Provo temple because he knew I'd feel his presence there, and all the moments when I'd imagined him still with me, shaking his head and laughing.

"Yes," I smiled softly. "I do."

I reflected on this conversation two months later during the Church's "Light the World" campaign. One of the challenges issued by the Church was to call our parents and tell them we love them.

My stomach churned as I read the invitation.

I wish so badly that I could call you, Dad, I thought miserably. *I wish I could tell you how much I love you.*

I could call my mother, at least. I did that, and I considered my task for the day to be done. But that afternoon, as I walked back towards my apartment after class, I distinctly heard my dad's voice. I was on the sidewalk south of the Harris Fine Arts Center, and I stopped in my tracks—it sounded like he was there in person, right next to me.

"Call Grandma Nancy," Dad said. "That's what I would do."

ONE BREATH AT A TIME

Oh, I thought. *That really* is *what you would do.*

He was so good about remembering to call his parents, his siblings, his friends. I have memories of him putting me on the phone with my grandparents at an early age to practice, even if I didn't know what to say. He taught us how important it is to stay in contact with and check in on the people you love.

So, as I began to walk towards my apartment once more, I called my Grandma Nancy.

She answered with a cheery, albeit confused, hello. I hesitated, unsure of what I was supposed to say. Finally, I decided to just tell the truth.

"Today's 'Light the World' prompt is to call your parents and tell them how much you love them," I choked up. "And I know Dad would have called you and told you how much he loves and appreciates you today, so I wanted to call and let you know that."

I told her how much we all love her. Both of us were teary before too long.

I walked around campus for the thirty minutes we talked. I looked up at the fluffy clouds and took in the pink-streaked sky behind the silhouette of the Hinckley Building.

When we had said goodbye and my phone was back in my backpack, I spun around and took everything in in slow motion—the soft sky, the blue mountains, the ridges of campus buildings and apartments. I felt so much peace, even inside of that missing, because I knew that my dad was still guiding me along. I knew that he was still touching my life for good.

What a striking contrast that experience was from my mindset earlier that summer. I remembered the day in June when I'd vented my anger to my Church history trip advisers

Beckee and Mandi, two sisters who had lost their dad when they were young.

"Everyone keeps saying that they feel my dad here with us, but I don't feel him here!" I cried. "Why do they get to feel him here and I don't? Why do they keep saying they can feel him here holding my hand or walking around with us? What does that even mean? Where is he?"

"You'll learn to feel him with you," Mandi said. "It just takes time. Be patient with yourself. You'll start seeing him with you everywhere you go."

"It's true," Beckee smiled. "My dad came on my mission with me. He still knows you. He's still with you. Just give it time."

And it was true. Just like that temple worker stopping during my confirmations to ask if the ordinances we were performing were for family members, there is evidence of spiritual presences everywhere we go. We can feel our ancestors with us helping us with our family history, guiding us through hard choices, and protecting us. The more we reach out to them and learn of their courage, the greater the impact they can have on our lives.

Back on campus, still savoring my conversation with my grandma and enjoying the spirit of peace that had come over me, I smiled as I began to walk home. I thought back to my conversation with Amber about how our connections with our loved ones continue to grow even after they pass away, how they become angels we can feel beside us.

"Always there are those angels who come and go all around us, seen and unseen, known and unknown, mortal

ONE BREATH AT A TIME

and immortal," Jeffrey R. Holland said.[1] "[God sends] angels, divine messengers, to bless His children, reassure them that heaven [is] always very close and that His help [is] always very near."

It's true, Dad, I told him, looking at the world through fresh eyes. *You knew me before. But you know me so much better now.*

---

1. Jeffrey R. Holland, "The Ministry of Angels," *Ensign*, November 2008.

Flashbacks

There have been lots of flashbacks. Big and small, sometimes bearable and sometimes not. But there was one horrible night in fall 2019 when I went to bed early but couldn't sleep for hours and hours. I was irritable, tossing and turning, my mind racing. 11:00 p.m. Midnight. 1:00 a.m.

Horrible, vivid flashbacks pulsed through my brain. My stomach churned. A tangible ache spread through my chest.

He's on the floor.

He's gray and stiff, lying in the casket.

The distended belly. The broken ribs.

His green eyes looking up, seeing nothing, seeing everything . . .

"If you go in the kitchen, take your butcher knife, and slice down each of your forearms, it won't hurt anymore," my OCD told me. Loudly. Clearly. "Just a quick compulsion. These obsessions can go away just like that. If you cut—and make sure it's symmetrical—the flashbacks will go away."

I knew it wasn't rational. But OCD isn't rational. And the promise of being free from flashbacks sounded too good to be true.

Really? I asked myself in a trance. *Will it go away? Is that all it takes?*

I imagined myself walking into the kitchen and opening the utensil drawer . . .

A panic rose in my throat.

No, that's not me. I don't want to do that. No, no, no—

"Heavenly Father, I'm scared, and I can't do this on my own," I finally prayed. "I don't want to hurt myself. That's not me, that's my OCD. I don't want to hurt myself. I know that won't fix this. Please, please, please help me to just be able to go to sleep. I'm so tired and scared. Please help me to fall asleep."

I lay there, paralyzed. I thought about phoning a hotline or calling out for my roommates, but I knew that if I were to move in any direction, even just to reach out for my phone, my instinct would be to go for the knives in the kitchen. So I just lay there, immobilized, and I prayed, and I prayed, and I prayed . . .

And finally, finally, I fell asleep.

When I woke up the next morning in a disheveled array of sheets and blankets, my arms were intact. Smooth. Unharmed.

I didn't feel that way on the inside, though. I felt gnarled and broken and bloody. It was terrifying to be paralyzed by something so foreign to me. An invisible enemy. A silent killer working from the inside, trying to convince me that it knew me better than I knew myself, trying to make me act against what I valued most.

As I later talked with a friend who was also experiencing flashbacks over life trauma, I was struck by an insight I hadn't considered before.

"I think flashbacks and whatnot are just our brains' way of processing hard things in our lives!" I texted her. "Maybe we just have to lean into the hard stuff. That's how we grow and get better."

It struck me that I could treat my struggle with flashbacks the same way I do my OCD. I started practicing exposure response prevention, or ERP, every time a flashback took over me. I picked a fear, and I leaned into it, facing it little by little until it had no power over me anymore. Until I knew I was free—or if not free, that I could at least survive it.

It's like a paper finger trap: You have to relax and lean in to loosen it enough for it to let you go. You have to accept the horrors of your brain and lean into the sorrow. You have to teach your brain that it's not so scary after all, that as much as you appreciate its defense mechanisms, they're doing you more harm than good right now.

And then they let you go.

We face our struggles again and again until the pain goes away. Like weightlifting, we start with the small things. We lift the scary memories into our minds and then we put them down again. Lift, and let them go. Feel the pain, and let it go. We move on to heavier and heavier weights.

Dad's body on the floor.

Lift. Let it go.

He wasn't in there anymore. He was gone. He didn't have to feel most of that. God can heal that broken body. He will be okay.

Lift. Let it go.

He's safe now. He's not hurting anymore. But all that blood, and those broken ribs . . . oh . . . oh . . . oh . . .

I lift and I exhale and I let it go.

Someday we will all have grown so much from facing our

traumas that we will hardly recognize our past selves—bruised, timid, afraid.

We will become more resilient than we ever imagined we could be.

Too Sensitive

I go for a run around the BYU campus, and I hear sirens racing down 900 East. My heart begins to race. My stomach tightens.

It's my brother, I think. *Or a friend. Is it my roommate? Are my roommates okay? It's someone I love, and they're hurt.*

I'm too terrified to move. I stop there on the sidewalk and shake as the horror sinks in. I'm not merely imagining the possibilities—I'm playing them out in real time, petrified.

And then, when the panic is over, I am left standing on the sidewalk, small and exhausted, angry that it has been seven months and I am still so afraid.

(I keep expecting the healing to go faster than it does. I forget how far I've already come, and I lose sight of how hard this trial genuinely is.)

But I pick up my feet again. I realize how strong I am to keep running when I couldn't before. I see how caring I am to think of others and to love them so deeply.

And I know that this too shall pass.

My brother Taylor and I go to a concert in northern Utah in fall 2019. As the singer performs onstage, videos that complement the songs play on the screen hanging behind him. At one point in the show, an image of a coffin comes up.

And suddenly it all comes rushing back. I remember what I have spent the past few months blocking out from my memory: My dad's discolored, waxy face. The white temple clothes. The stiff hands.

I freeze.

Oh, no, I think. *Not here. Not now.*

But rather than let that flashback consume me, I decide to refocus.

Instead of thinking about Dad in a coffin, I tell myself, *I'm going to picture him jumping next to us in this mosh pit.*

He came to this exact venue in the 90s. I picture him as a college student with a mullet and a jean jacket, grinning ear to ear, jumping up and down beside me.

Driving home afterwards, it strikes me just how much of a difference it made for me to change the associations I was making in my mind. It was difficult at first, but I know that with practice, it will get easier and come more naturally.

Whether or not there are sirens to fill me with fear, I am seized with endless strains of anxiety every time I go running at BYU during those first few months. Horrible, intrusive thoughts took over my mind—

Your heart is beating too fast. You're dying. You're not healthy. You're going to die, right here, right now.

You can run as fast as you want, but you can't outrun everything that hurts you. You can't outrun dying. You can't outrun that you're the reason your dad is dead.

You're going to die just like he did, and there's nothing you can do to stop it. This is all your fault. This is what you deserve.

Those thoughts slam into me like a train. Drained of energy, I blink back tears and stumble back to my apartment.

But there is finally a run when that all changes. I'm south of BYU campus, striding along the sidewalk adjacent to the duck pond, when the voice comes into my head again.

You're going to die just like your dad did, Gabrielle. There's nothing you can do to stop it, no matter how fast you run.

I mull those painful words over in my mind, and I finally reply, *Okay. Maybe. Maybe I will. But I'm going to do everything in my power to keep going, anyway. I'm going to focus only on what I have control over. I don't have to worry about the rest.*

I keep running, and the voice stays away for some time.

But there is always something new to be afraid of. My friend spends too long underwater after tipping her canoe, and I think she has drowned. My neighbor's daughter is missing, and I imagine her in a ditch. My roommate doesn't text me back while on a date and I'm afraid I'm already too late, that her killer is already getting away. I hear sirens again and again and am seized with chest-tightening, nauseating, excruciating fear.

It does not go away. It's PTSD and OCD collaborating against my brain, having a field day on my emotions.

It is not easy. But I am learning to lean into it. I am learning to say, "I am sensitive right now. And I hurt right now. But it is better now than it was a month ago, and when it is through, I will heal."

I have spent so much time wishing to be less sensitive, to hurt less, to feel less, to shield myself from all this pain. I get why people numb themselves to their emotions; it is scary to face this reality. But now, finally, I am realizing the truth:

I don't want to give up being sensitive. It is in this fragile, moldable state that my Savior can turn me into who He needs me to be. It is in this claylike stage that I can change and become anything I want to be. I can make it through this, one breath at a time.

It still hurts, you see, because it still matters. I still miss Dad because I still love him. Just like my seminary teacher Brother Holyoak taught me, "Mourning is the purest form of love." This sensitivity I feel is a form of love. This pain is part of the healing.

I'm finally, *finally* realizing that being sensitive is an enormous gift.

Sensitive to the Spirit.

Sensitive to the needs of others.

Sensitive to pain. And, most importantly—

Sensitive to *joy*.

A Different Kind of Missing

I started my first semester of college rooming with five strangers from across the United States. It was innocent on their part, but every time they mentioned their dads, my chest tightened. They talked about favorite memories they had with their fathers and how much they missed having them around. My mouth went dry every time. I had no idea how to confront that anguish.

You don't get it, I thought miserably. *You have no idea what it means to miss your dad. You get to call him. You get to go home at Thanksgiving and see him again.*

Every time they called their families, every time they talked about what they were doing, every time they recalled memories or plans they were making with their parents, my stomach churned. I felt sickened every time I was reminded of how incomplete our family was now. Every conversation was a brand-new heartbreak.

But by the end of that semester, something changed. My roommates didn't talk about their dads any less, and I didn't feel any less pain over the loss of my own father. But there was one late night around midnight when I realized how much I had grown and how many triggers I was finally able to tolerate that would have once driven me to my knees.

ONE BREATH AT A TIME

It was right before finals week. Bleary-eyed, drowsy, and stumbling, we brushed our teeth and said good night in the middle of the hallway before heading off to bed.

"We're going home so soon!" one commented, leaning on the doorframe. "Man, I miss my dad."

"I do, too," another sighed.

"Me, too," I chimed in, straight-faced. And they all looked at me, realizing the significance of what I'd said, and laughed. Finally, I joined in and laughed, too.

It is a different kind of missing, I realized.

It is learning to remember the good and let it wash away the bad. It is learning to be sweet again instead of bitter, vulnerable instead of guarded. To let humor and light fill the cracks in my soul. To not be angry when others misspeak, to not expect them to be sensitive to my every trauma.

I can choose not to be offended. I can choose to be soft. I can choose to let go and let God.

There is a strange, hollow place inside of me that is beginning, ever so slowly, to heal.

The Jolt

I was home from college for two weeks for Christmas break. Late one night, as I drove into the garage, I glanced over to the front of the house where Dad always parked his truck.

Huh, I thought. *Dad isn't home yet. His truck isn't here.*

And then it hit me like an avalanche.

I had forgotten, for that brief, blissful moment, that he was gone. That horrible realization swept me under, churned in my stomach, suffocated me.

"He's gone," I whispered, tears coming to my eyes. "Oh, he's really gone."

I do it again and again. I see a white truck pull up next to me at a gas station and wonder if he's inside. I take a cute picture of my little brothers and start drafting a text so I can send it to him (I don't think I'll ever be able to delete his contact information from my phone). It is still so surreal to me that I keep forgetting he's truly gone. It is impossible to imagine that there is a reality worth living in that doesn't have him by my side.

It's worse when I'm dreaming. Somehow, my subconscious has yet to realize he's gone. In every dream I have, he's in it, and he's alive, and everything is good. We're going on family vacations. He's coming with me on an adventure. We're together.

*Our family in November 2016.
From left: Kenji, Taylor, Dad, Sam, Mom, me.*

Speaking of sleeping, you know the precarious balance between sleeping and waking, the moment when your legs jolt out from under you, startled, throwing you back into consciousness?

Sometimes life feels like that bad dream, that precarious balance. I'm constantly being jolted in and out of wakefulness, of reality. I am jolted in and out of that truth over and over again—

My dad is not coming home.

I've lost him. My confidante. My adventure buddy. My mentor. My father. I didn't even get to say goodbye. I didn't even get to hold his hand.

There is a logical side of grief. This is the side that reminds you that you can heal. It assures you that because of Christ, you'll see your family again someday. You'll be reunited, made whole. There's the reality of angels and temples and life after death.

But Christ wept with Mary and Martha before He healed Lazarus (see John 11:35). There is still an emotional side of grief, a side that jolts you awake again and again. This side cannot be drowned out by logic, for it is a weeping voice that demands to be heard.

I am comforted by the knowledge that my Savior bore my pain so that He could understand what it feels like to hurt this badly.

"Surely he hath borne our griefs, and carried our sorrows," Isaiah testified (Isaiah 53:4).

He knows how it feels to not get the chance to say goodbye.

He knows the pain of feeling completely alone.

He understands the jolting pain of forgetting and then remembering that they're gone.

He knows how hard it was to miss His Heavenly Father and to be away from Him for so long. He knows the struggle of being away from His dad.

I can live in the jolt for as long as it takes, for I know He's in it with me. Someday, sooner than I know, reality will look sweeter again. The jolt will ease. I won't be in so much pain anymore.

Someday, I won't have to say goodbye ever again.

You Don't Have to Be Good at This

"I just feel like I should be doing better than I am," I sighed. I crossed my arms and stared out the window at the frosty January world. "I'm just so frustrated and burnt out and sad. Shouldn't I be doing better than this? Shouldn't I be struggling less? I feel like I've already worked through so much of my grief and learned so many things about taking care of my mental health, but it just doesn't get better."

My newest therapist contemplates my words.

"Everybody has problems," I add. "I should be able to just . . . *deal* with this."

"Have you thought about the fact that you've never been in these circumstances before?" she asks, tilting her head. "Sure, other people have hard things they're going through too. But not a lot of people are dealing with trauma and grief from losing their dad AND OCD symptoms flaring up AND a hard semester at college AND dating stress. This is an unprecedented combination for you. Maybe you don't have to be good at this."

"But I want to be," I argue. "I've been doing this long enough. I should know better."

"Gabrielle." She leans forward and looks me in the eye. "You have never been here before, and you will never be here again. You are in this moment. Right now. You are missing your dad. You aren't getting enough sleep. You're overworked. It's winter. You're struggling with a new semester. You might need to try medication. There's a lot to figure out.

"But you won't ever have to feel this exact set of emotions again about this exact set of problems. You can stop expecting yourself to know how to do this right," my therapist says, leaning back in her chair. "What if you just let yourself be where you are?"

I sit there with the discomfort, the imperfection, the "failure" of not knowing how to do this right.

And then those circumstances change, and I enter a new phase of life. The next challenge.

I move forward.

I do not have to be good at this.

I will never be in that exact set of circumstances again.

Road Trip

Mid-February, I bring my college friends Jocelyn and Trevor on a road trip to my hometown. I show them all the places I love most—the Inside Scoop, the best diner in the world; the *Progress* office where I wrote for our town newspaper; the hills I hiked and ran and explored.

Mom is working on selling our house so she can leave Moapa Valley. As much as it hurts me to watch her say goodbye to the town I'd spent the first eighteen years of my life in, I know how hard it is to still be in that great big empty house where something so devastating happened. I know how hard it is to be stuck in the past, physically and emotionally, spinning in a hamster wheel instead of moving forward.

So as much as I'm showing off our single McDonald's and our dusty hiking trails to my new friends, I'm also saying goodbye to Moapa Valley, because I don't know when I'll be back or if I'll ever live there again.

When my friends have their fill of Vegas lights and small-town wonders, we put a morning aside to help my mom work on packing up our house. The task she gives us is to fold my dad's shirts so we can put them in storage.

I'll never forget this tender experience. Jocelyn and Trevor and I sit on my parents' bedroom floor with stacks of shirts between us. I show them the way to fold them so that they'll all look the same—Marie Kondo–style, in thirds and then in half and then in thirds again so that they stand up on their own. I'm working quickly but gently, placing each folded shirt in a row in a storage tote. I keep glancing up to check on my friends' progress, though, because it is the sweetest and most sacred thing I've seen:

My friends, who have never met my dad, reverently fold the shirts he loves so that we can hold on to them and keep them in good condition. The respect and the love that they show for my dad and for me brings me to tears as I sit there with them on the carpet. They keep looking up at me to ask for my approval, to make sure they are folding the shirts just right. They pat down the sleeves in perfect creases. They lovingly lay the shirts in the box side by side.

What a special experience.

I just know Dad is going to love them when he meets them in the next life.

Remembering

 I keep remembering how I messed up. How the Spirit told me to take a picture of Dad jogging with Sam and I didn't. How He insisted and I dug in my heels. How that image is fading from my memory and someday I won't remember how it looked the last time the sun shone on him. I hate that I messed that up. I hate that. I'm so mad at myself. I hate that I can't ever fix that, that I didn't follow that prompting, that I don't have that photo and I never recorded the sound of his laugh and that all of those important memories are already slipping away from me.
 It haunts me.

So, So Much

The pandemic hits, and our world turns upside down. BYU moves its classes online. My mom has just sold her house and is temporarily moving in with her parents in Washington while she works on figuring out where to move next. My peers and I scramble as we try to make sense of our new circumstances.

Should we stay in our dorms? Should we go home?

Will this be over in a week? In a month? Can it really take any longer than that?

But we don't have to make decisions just yet. That first weekend, before anything else, my friend Mikayla takes a group of friends to her family's place, and I come with her.

We don't have to worry about the future just yet. For now, we can go make memories.

And we do. We stay up late watching movies and discussing all the trivia and behind-the-scenes secrets that make them even more fun. We watch *Contagion* and speculate about the pandemic, because it's early enough that it still doesn't feel real, and with all of us safe and tucked away from the world, it feels like COVID-19 can't possibly affect us. We dance in the living room and walk barefoot in the snow, flip confetti pancakes in the kitchen and go sledding in the backyard. We pull an all-nighter to watch the sunrise. We live.

During the all-nighter, I chat with my friend Mikayla and her friend Matt, who I do not know well. The three of us are determined to stay up through the whole night.

We ask each other deep questions about what we want out of life and what we have learned so far from being human. We have the kind of conversations you cannot have at any time other than at 3:00 a.m., the kind where you don't look into each other's eyes and just exist side by side instead. We share our favorite songs and our biggest struggles, and I finally tell them about the big burden weighing on my heart: my dad's death. I have not been talking about it lately, haven't let anyone into that corner of my mind, and that grief seems to be growing in me. Expanding. Ready to burst unless I let it out.

I am not asking for a pity party—I am being vulnerable with them. And Matt responds in a way I do not anticipate but will never forget:

He tells me about how tough his Church mission was. He whispers loving stories into the dark night about all the people he met, and I listen as I gaze out the windows into the gentle darkness.

"I met so many people I didn't know how to help," Matt whispers. "There are so many tough things out there that people experience. Like you losing your dad. I met so many struggling people out there. There are just some things you can't fix. You can't even try."

We aren't looking into each other's eyes. Instead, we are seeing the same shadowed ceiling, the same quiet night. We are strangers who have never talked before, sharing secrets in the middle of the night.

"But what I could tell them is just how much Heavenly Father loves them," Matt murmurs. "I just got to testify to them how loving God is. And He really is. He loves us so, so much."

He whispers those last few words so fervently that tears begin welling in my eyes.

"Do you know that?" he whispers. "Gabrielle, I don't know you that well, but I want you to know that Heavenly Father knows you. He knows *you*. And He loves you so, so much."

We are surrounded not just by soft darkness now but by love too, love that permeates into every corner of the room and fills my heart with a peace it has not felt in quite some time. I am flooded by this simple yet powerful conversation about God's love, about healing, about the struggles of being human . . . all with someone I have never talked to before.

I am sitting here in the middle of this uncertainty, and I am sitting in God's love, too.

The outside world slowly lightens, and we make our way out onto the porch to watch the sunrise. We huddle in blankets against the cold, shifting from one frozen foot to the other, leaning over the icy railing to the pink skies and tiny red houses below us. We find shapes in the clouds and watch the sky turn peach and apricot-colored.

And now that moment is no more, but it exists forever in that snapshot in my mind. That perfect sequence of staying up all night to see something beautiful happen. That tenderly whispered conversation about the love of God permeating everything around and within us.

I had no idea what would happen next with the pandemic, with the school year, with my family, with my grief. I was suffocated by uncertainty.

But that weekend at the cabin I was beginning to learn that life goes on when everything around us changes. There is still goodness everywhere. There are kind people all over. There is nature and music and laughter, and there are nights where you stay up late with someone you have never spoken with before to talk about the spiritual moments that have changed your life.

And there is God.

And He is good.

Journal Entry: Exactly How It's Supposed to Be

March 26, 2020

Trying to finish up my semester online while living with my family at my grandparents' house in Washington isn't going so well. It's hard to focus and find quiet time to study. I'm having a hard time learning these days.

But one thing I do love about being here is being able to explore nature. I've been going on walks on my own, and I find that I can hear God the clearest I've ever been able to. I went on a walk tonight in the cool of evening after dinner, taking everything in with absolute wonder and delight. I prayed as I walked, telling Heavenly Father that I've been thinking about my dad and that I love and miss him.

Immediately the impression came to me that I wouldn't have the opportunity to write this book and learn all these lessons and help so many people if Dad were still here. I wouldn't be able to grow the ways I have. I would have been like Adam and Eve stuck in the Garden of Eden. I needed this trial to be able to progress.

It was an uncomfortable feeling. It boggled my mind. But I sat with it and finally found that it was true.

He's proud of you, the Spirit whispered.

I sure hope he is, I sighed.

ONE BREATH AT A TIME

But I kept walking and contemplating, and I saw how everything around me was an expression of God's love for us. He is so, so good. I see Him in the beautiful green trees and in the cute middle-aged couple I saw going out for a run together. I see Him in the trials we go through and the peace we feel through Him. I see Him everywhere.

My life is a gift. My life has a plan.

I have so many things to write and such a great work to do.

Everywhere around me in nature is a temple. I miss being in temples. I miss proxy baptisms and confirmations and the beautiful artwork and the comforting Spirit. But I looked around at all of nature today and worshipped Heavenly Father and tried to figure out how to understand His plan, and as I did so I realized that everywhere I go can be made holy.

He is here.

He is everywhere.

He is in the pain I am feeling, and He is in the purpose that I am making out of my pain.

Tonight, Mom and my brothers and I said family prayer together on the carpet in the stairwell. When it was over we all just collapsed into each other and laughed, and we stayed there for a long time. We played with each other's hair and hugged each other and giggled for a long, long time. We *lived* together. It was the kind of moment you miss even as you're still experiencing it.

This is not what I thought my life would look like.

Yet this is exactly how it is supposed to be.

2:00 a.m.

"Hey, Conner," I whisper into the phone one night in April. "Can we talk?"

"Gabrielle, it's two in the morning," my friend groans. "What's going on? Are you okay?"

I pause for a moment, knowing how ridiculous my request is going to sound.

"Can you . . . tell me about how bugs work? Like how they say that bugs eat you after you die?"

"What?" Conner asks. "What even are you talking about?"

"You know," I say. "They talk about how we give our bodies back to the earth, you know? And there are little bugs that eat you and turn you into dirt. I just can't sleep because I'm worried about that."

"Why are you worried about that?"

"Well . . . bugs are probably eating my dad's body," I trembled. "And I really, really don't like that."

Conner explains to me that the bugs that eat us when we die are just helpful little microorganisms that already lived on our skin; there's nothing scary or new that comes to eat us if we're buried right.

"WHAT?" I demand. My initial concern has nearly been abated, but now there's a new worry on my mind. "Tell me more about these microorganisms. You're telling me WHAT is on my skin?"

But it turns out microorganisms aren't quite as creepy as I thought they were. They mostly just eat our dead skin cells. And then they eat us when we die. No biggie. It even turns out that life as we know it wouldn't be possible without the bacteria and fungi that break down dead organisms in the wild.

That seems a lot less scary than what I was imagining happening to my dad. And to my eyelashes.

"Now do you think you'll fall asleep?" Conner asks.

"Maybe," I say.

And I do.

Journal Entry: One Year

May 3, 2020

This May 3rd was a lot better than last May 3rd, but I suppose that isn't hard to beat.

Still, I was surprised by how much peace accompanied this day. I woke up feeling slightly miserable as my mind flooded with reminders of all my inadequacies as a daughter and all the ways I had failed Dad.

Remember when he sat on the floor in Sunday School and asked you to come join him, but you wouldn't because you thought he looked silly?

Remember when he wanted to take you home from your quiz team competition but you went home with the team instead?

Remember when you made him cry?

"Oh, dear Heavenly Father," I pleaded. "I know I didn't do this right. I'm so sorry. I wish I could go back and do it the right way. But please just tell my dad that I love him."

I tried my best to snap out of it.

No, I reminded myself fiercely. *There are still so many things we did right. There are still so many things that were good.*

I may not get a do-over, but I do *get a do-better.*

The day got better. Little by little. There were so many tender mercies and so many people who reached out.

There was time in the sunshine. There were phone calls with my friend Jocelyn and my Grandma Nancy. Jocelyn made me laugh, boosting my spirits, and my grandma reminded me what a tender mercy it was that Dad died at home surrounded by people he loved instead of at his workplace or in his truck or at a hospital.

Little things.

It's the little things that count.

Taylor and I went on a drive tonight and shared Sour Patch Kids. Sam fell asleep on my window seat tonight while I stroked his soft, blond hair. My cousin Hailey and I made cheesy garlic biscuits, and the lemon bars I baked—one of dad's favorite treats—turned out better than they ever had before.

Playing ping-pong upstairs with my boy cousins. Sitting on the back porch with bare feet in the warm sunshine. The best hugs.

Above all else, the biggest joy of today has been having the chance to reflect on all the ways I've grown in the past year. I marvel at how much more resilient I am, how much more joy and appreciation I feel, how much stronger my relationship is with my Heavenly Father.

So, yes. This May 3rd was much better than last year's.

But I'm grateful for both of them. I'm grateful for every breath I get to take.

I'm grateful that I get to keep going, for who knows what I will have learned a year from now?

What I've Gained

Tenacity
An increased fervor for life
Gratitude for every breath I get to take
A testimony of my Savior's
Atonement like never before
More love for my family
Hope. And hope. And hope again.
More purpose in striving for exaltation
A deeper love for my Heavenly Father
Perspective and empathy
And, most of all—
My guardian angel.
Here, right beside me.
Guiding me
Along.

Roses and Hydrangeas

It's the Saturday before Mother's Day, and I'm racing up and down the aisles of Costco, working on putting together the finishing touches on what I hope will be the perfect scavenger hunt for Mom.

Dad, you should be here, I grumble as I pick out a canister of chocolate-covered almonds. I think about the piteous Mother's Day we'd had last year in the aftermath of Dad's death. *I don't know how to make this stuff fun. You're the one that always did such a great job.*

I stop at a flower stand and take in the variety of Mother's Day florals on display. A bundle of roses or a bouquet of hydrangeas? I take one in each hand and look back and forth, my brow furrowing.

Roses are traditional, I think. *But she loves hydrangeas too. Which one should I get? Which one will be more special?*

"Both," Dad says with a wink.

It's strange. I look around as if I'll actually see him standing beside me. I can hear him in my head and can vividly see his smiling, winking face.

"Get both," Dad says with a grin and a shrug. "Why not?"

So I do. I buy the hydrangeas *and* the roses. I trim them when I get home, arrange them in vases, then hide them in my closet for the next day. Hydrangeas from me. Roses from Dad. It's perfect.

My parents in a photo booth, summer 1997.

That night, sitting around a campfire with aunts and uncles, I feel ready for the holiday ahead. My alarm is set, my prizes are ready, my clues are printed and stacked in my drawer.

I make my mom a perfect s'more like Dad taught me—slow-cooked, light and golden, soft and gooey.

"Dad's proud," Mom smiles through a bite of graham cracker.

And that's exactly what I need to hear.

Fifty

May 27, 2020

    Dear Dad,

    Happy birthday! Fifty would have looked good on you.

    Someday we'll go on rollercoasters again and dance to Chubby Checker. But for now I just hope they still eat key lime pie in Paradise.

    I miss you.

    After how touching and beautiful the one-year anniversary was, I was expecting an equally tranquil birthday. But not being able to celebrate with you was so hard. We performed a service activity in the morning because you were always doing something to serve someone. We were scouring the store for the perfect toys to donate when I came across a jumbo pack of self-tying water balloons, just like the ones you bought for girls' camp. Remember those? Those were so fun. So silly. So *you*. It felt like you were there with me, helping me pick them out.

    But the day got harder and harder as my emotions wore me down. I was exhausted from missing you, angry at myself for not dealing with your loss better, devastated that grief wasn't getting any easier, panicked that I wasn't accomplishing enough. I finally broke down on the dock outside my uncle's house, tears streaming down my face, trying to decide if I could keep going or not. My OCD worked my thoughts into a tightening spiral, casting dark shadows on everything around me. It reminded me how far I was away from where I wanted to be, how I'd messed up in irredeemable ways, how my life was too hard to be worth living, yet I simultaneously was not good enough to be alive.

Then I remembered I was supposed to have a video call with my friend Ashlynn and her missionary companion. I didn't feel up to talking, but I sat up anyway and dialed into the call. I dropped my feet over the edge of the dock and let them kick in the water. Wiping my tears from my eyes, I listened as the Spirit began to fill me in the most powerful way it had in quite some time.

Dad, Ashlynn had no idea. I don't know if she remembered what today was. She didn't know how hard I was being on myself or how my OCD was tearing me down.

But do you know what we talked about?

Hope. Fending off discouragement. Living day by day, trusting God. Finding joy. Those were the topics she and her companion chose.

Ashlynn read from the scriptures, "Your heavenly Father knoweth [what] ye have need of. . . . Take therefore no thought for the morrow: for the morrow shall take thought for the things of itself" (Matthew 6: 32, 34).

I didn't need to fret about how I was going to make it through the next few months or even through the next week. I didn't need to punish myself for everything I hadn't accomplished yet or everything I thought I'd done wrong. I just had to focus on today. I just had to take this one breath at a time.

When my days make me weaker, God's love grows stronger to make up the difference. When I fall apart, he is ready to put me back together. Whatever my day demands of me, God will support me, will strengthen me, will make up for what I lack.

"He's not going to give you anything that's too hard for you to do with His help," Ashlynn said. "You don't need to worry about getting it all right. God knows what you need day by day. You can just trust that He will provide a way."

It's not just about the words they said or the hymn we sang. It's about the spirit I felt out there on the dock, even as those missionaries were hundreds of miles away from me, testifying to me that it was going to be okay. It's about the spark of hope that came alive in my soul again.

God sent me those missionaries, Dad. And then he sent me one of my high school teachers, who emailed me a kind message and told me she had felt impressed to reach out to me. He sent me a friend who texted to check in without even knowing the significance of the date. He sent me s'mores and a campfire and the prettiest sunset I'd ever seen.

He sent me my Uncle Sean, who told me today, "You're awesome. Your mom and brothers are lucky to have you. I just want you to know that."

I felt like such a burden, like I wasn't doing enough, but his words were exactly what I needed to hear. They softened my soul.

I'm too hard on myself.
I let the devil work in me.
I let discouragement take hold on my heart.

The reality is that someday I'll enjoy your birthdays again

and someday we'll go on drives together again and someday I will have grown so much I'll hardly recognize my past self. Who knows what waits ahead for us?

For now, I just have the assurance that you're nearby and that you're safe. Above all, I have the assurance that God loves me, and He loves you, and it's all going to be okay. I know that we're doing enough. That trying our best is enough.

And for now, in this moment, this knowledge is all I need.

Love,
Gabrielle

You Will

You think you will never feel joy again.
But you will.

You will feel euphoria at
Niagara Falls. Drenched
In spray, mouth gaping wide, and laughing.
You will eat buttered popcorn at movie theaters
And laugh your heart out with your friends.

You will hold a sleeping baby in your lap
And will lick cookie dough ice cream
as it drips down your wrist.
You will go boating at sunset
and watch the sherbet sky
Turn the turquoise waters into
golden, rippling art.

There will be sunshine.
You will bask in it.
The light will come through again, and
You will wrap your fingers
around a new kind of joy.

You will live again. Better. More fully.
Not in spite of what you've lost
But because of it—for the dichotomy
You now know, for the despair and the joy.

GABRIELLE SHIOZAWA

You are hurting, my dear, but you will heal.
You will feel peace, even inside
Of this pain.

For you will come to know your
Savior better
Than you ever did
Before.

You will feel the complex joy
Of being human
In its fullest.

You are learning, now,
What it means to fall apart.
You will learn, soon enough,
How Christ puts you back
Together.

I know it is impossible to imagine
Feeling joy again
When the hurt runs so deeply
You can hardly
Breathe.

But, I promise you—
You will.

It Is Enough

My friend Morgan came home from her mission in July 2020, and we celebrated being together again after spending eighteen months apart. From cooking authentic Italian lasagna with her to even just being able to hug her again, it was the sweetest reunion I could have imagined.

I wondered how she would broach the topic of my dad. Maybe we would delve into heartbreaking conversations, but maybe she'd just tiptoe around his memory. I wasn't sure what to expect, or even what I wanted.

But she didn't start an awkward conversation with me about what it was like to lose Dad or interview me about how I've grieved and how I've grown. We'd done enough of that already in the emails we'd exchanged. Instead, Morgan did something even better: She perfectly inserted my dad into conversations whenever possible.

"Remember that picture you sent me of your dad jumping up and down in a parking garage?" Morgan laughed. "That's the funniest photo—remind me of that story?"

She reminded me that my dad always made her feel like she was a part of our family. Scrolling through old texts, she said, "Which emojis did he pick to represent your family members? I think I was a bear. You were a ghost, Taylor was a slice of pizza . . ."

No painful conversations. No adding insult to injury. We just remembered all the good. We talked about the honest emotions, the good and the bad. The grief and the growth. By sharing these memories, by not shying away from mentioning him, Morgan is helping to keep my dad alive. He feels close again. It's like he's on a mission now, just like she was. I'll see him so, so soon, and the reunion will be even sweeter than the one I'd just had with Morgan.

I used to think that Church missions seemed so long, that it was unbearable to be away from someone for up to two years while they served the Lord. I laugh as I remember how dramatically I mourned when my brother left on his mission. But now I know that absence truly does make the heart grow fonder. I know Morgan and I have a richer friendship for having grown separately and for being reunited once more. I know that someday all the days I've spent missing Dad will just be distant memories, because he'll be with me again, and because even now I still have his memories and his love here with me. I'll tell him about all these adventures I have for the rest of my life, and he'll say, "I know, Boo—I was there with you."

One of the nights I was staying with Morgan, we piled into a truck with her siblings and drove out to Red Rock to stargaze. We scaled the dusty orange rock formations and settled in to wait for the stars to come out.

And then the perfect moment happened. One of those cinematic moments. Everyone was talking and laughing. "Rose" by Honest Men was playing on Morgan's phone. Morgan sat there, illuminated by the setting sun, the darkening ridges of

ONE BREATH AT A TIME

Red Rock growing dim around and behind her. I looked at my friend sitting next to me. She was glowing.

I don't have the answers. I don't know what the future looks like. I still haven't made perfect sense of my past, I thought. *But I'm here now, and I'm with my friend who I love, and I feel joy and peace like I've never felt before.*

"And that's enough," the Spirit whispered. "That's enough."

I thought back to the picture I didn't take. May 3. Sam and Dad running in the setting sun. I was so upset with myself for letting that memory go.

But I know now that it's not just about having tangible evidence of a moment I love. I don't have to video everything. Not everything has to be captured. Sometimes it's enough to have the memories, the emotions, the experiences. Because those stay in your heart, lingering on your skin, long after they've passed. It is enough to remember that I sat there looking at my friend and thought about how much I loved her and how joyful I felt in that moment. It is enough to remember riding roller coasters with my dad and feeling safe and exhilarated all at once. It is enough to experience it and not have to capture it forever, to cradle the white butterfly in the net and then to let it go free.

And right here, right now, right where I am, is enough.

Journal Entry: More White Butterflies

September 15, 2020

During the first part of the COVID-19 pandemic, March through August, my family and I spent nearly six entire months house-hunting. We lived out of hotels, rentals, and friends' and relatives' basements in Washington, Idaho, Nevada, and Utah. It was crazy, uncertain, exhausting, and endurance-building. Half our stuff was in storage and the other half was stuffed into the back of our cars. I had no idea where we were going to end up next.

But eventually the pieces clicked together. We found a house. I found an apartment for school. We took everything out of storage.

And finally it was September, and we were all in Provo. Together. We got the keys to the house just six days ago. I'm exhausted. Our lives are going nothing like I thought they would. Yet I think they are just as they are supposed to be. As hard as everything has been, as challenging and uncertain as these past few months have been, today we all celebrated Sam's birthday. Together. As I looked around at the soft sunshine illuminating my mom's new backyard, at my little brothers giggling while jumping on their trampoline, at my family existing together here, I thought how grateful I am for all we are learning about adaptation and resilience and hope. I thought about how grateful I am to be alive at all, to exist here in this moment at this time.

Just as I was pondering the hollow place I wish Dad was filling in our celebration, I looked up in time to see a kaleidoscope of white butterflies rising from the bushes in our yard.

Hi, Dad, I thought with a smile. *Of course you're still here. Of course.*

I'm going to lean into the challenges. Lean into trusting God's timing. Lean into all the lessons and love and life I will experience along the way.

I promise there is a silver lining on every single raincloud.

Reservoirs of Joy

I am sitting on a swing in my aunt and uncle's backyard in Pocatello, Idaho, in fall 2020. My cousins and brothers are laughing and chasing each other through the deep green grass, crunching through yellow leaves. The whole world seems to slow around me as I stop and think for a moment.

I look back on a past version of myself who, two years earlier, grumbled and complained as she came to Idaho to visit "ill-acquainted relatives" she now adores. I look back on the girl who didn't want to hear "boring old stories" from her dad who now sits by her grandpa's side to ask him questions and listen to him talk. I look at that anxious and hurting seventeen-year-old, and I ache for all she did not understand. But I marvel, too, at how much I have grown and experienced since then. I marvel at how much bigger and brighter my world has become, how much color and wonder my dad still adds to my corner of the universe.

I look around at all these relatives I love. Grandma and Mom and Aunt Ali are talking in the kitchen; I can see them through the window. Taylor and Uncle Matt and Grandpa are laughing about something by the grill. The little kids are shrieking and laughing with breathless exhilaration as they chase each other around in the grass. There is so much life and color that is still ours to hold.

The words of a refrain I once heard come to mind: "Righteous sorrow and suffering carve cavities in the soul that will become later reservoirs of joy."

Reservoirs of joy. It has been seventeen months since we lost Dad, but I can feel peace seeping into these cavities in my soul, drop by drop. I think about how Dad used to send me articles about kintsugi, the Japanese art of putting broken pottery back together using gold. I marvel at how embracing this difficult part of my life has helped me become stronger. This trial has taken away part of me, but it has replaced that part with gold. I am being repaired, renewed, reinvigorated. This reservoir in my heart is being filled with a new kind of joy.

This joy looks like jumping on the trampoline with Sam and pretending to be dinosaurs chasing each other. This looks like kissing my little cousins on their foreheads, like sitting with little Ivory to do puzzles and color, like stepping into the kitchen to help Grandma cook enchiladas. This joy looks like slowing down for a moment and sitting on this swing, watching the world spin, and realizing that I don't have to keep running to try to keep up with it.

I can be still.

I can be peaceful.

I can breathe.

And it is here, as I sit and reflect and kick my legs back and forth and rock through the cool October air, that I feel that reservoir of joy filling up.

Thank-You Notes

The easiest answers were driving too fast, screaming, punching walls, and hiding in my room . . . but there were some days when I found better outlets. One day, when the grief and the anger and the ache in my chest were all too much, I spent an afternoon writing thank-you notes. I wrote them to teachers I admired, to community members that had served my family, to friends who had lightened my burdens.

By the end of the day, as I looked back, I saw that I had still been sad that day, and I had still endured the discomfort and pain of grieving, but I had not been devastated. I had not suffered as much as I had on the days when I gave in to the darkness.

So yes, I was practicing gratitude for the sake of letting people know that I appreciated them. But at the same time, I was healing myself. I was showing myself how much good was still left in the world, how much I still had that I could be grateful for. I was telling God how grateful I was. I was soothing my tired and aching soul.

I took out my pen and another sheet of paper.

And I kept going.

And now, again, I say thank you. Thank you to everyone who said the things I needed to hear the most—"It's okay not to be okay right now" and "We don't have to have all the answers, we can just take it one day at a time" and "Do you need me to come over?"

To my teachers for caring, to everyone who sent thoughtful texts and reached out their arms in love. To everyone who came over to take care of our yard and wash our cars, who gave us priesthood blessings and hugged us and brought us food. To everyone who sanctified our pain, who showed us that angels do exist on this earth, who didn't try to rush us through our healing process.

To Dad, for a lifetime of memories and lessons and love. For seeing the best in me and making me want to be better. For showing me what a good life looks like. For that last run, for the ways you made me laugh, for the way you gave me so much to love.

To my Savior, for giving me what I needed instead of what I wanted. For loving me enough to break me. For molding me into who you need me to be.

The anguish still lingers here in the shadowed corners of my haunted house. The anger stomps in when I keep the door unlocked. I still look around and see empty chairs that cannot be filled and gaping wounds that this life cannot heal.

But I look around, too, at all I have left. At all the ways I've grown and all the growth that is yet to come, at all the wounds that have healed into scars. At all the joy I have yet to feel. At the promise of seeing Dad again someday.

This is more than enough.

Thank you.

Again

Sometimes I wake up and feel like I'm at the bottom of the Grand Canyon all over again. I'm looking up at all the miles and miles I have yet to climb, at more days of despair and heavyheartedness and grief. And I say, "Not again. Not another day. I cannot go through this anymore."

But I look around me at all the people who are in the canyon with me, at all those who have climbed this before, at those who have to run from one end of the canyon over and over again as they fight and grow and conquer through grief and disappointment and despair. I look at all the headlamps and maps that are guiding the way, the walking sticks I can lean on, the friends who are helping me along.

I look at my Savior, stretching out His hand. Beckoning me.

We still have so much farther to travel. It's true. It took me eighteen months to be able to dance to Chubby Checker's "Let's Twist Again" once more. I still find myself panicking that I have diabetes without knowing it, despite the medical tests that say otherwise, or that my heart is beating so fast it will give out.

I am not where I want to be. I don't know that any of us are—

ONE BREATH AT A TIME

But we have already come so far.

"We have done this before," we all say together. We hold on to each other's hands, straighten our shoulders, and take another step into the unknown.

"We can do this again."

Our family at the Provo City Center Temple, July 2020.
From left: Sam, me, Mom, Kenji, Taylor.

Dear Friend,

As my friend Beckee described it, "Welcome to the club of loss." It seems like a lonely place, doesn't it? Everyone here is experiencing an unprecedented loss or disappointment. Everyone has unique pains and anguishes and weaknesses. But the uniting factor is that every single person ends up here. To be alive, you see, is to be missing.

So, where do we go from here?

We share our stories. We lift each other up. We act as God's hands, and we dry each other's tears.

Right now, you may still be Peter the man, faltering on the water. But as you grow through your pain, as you lean on your Savior and allow Him to sanctify your sorrow, you can grow into Peter the Apostle, who reaches down a hand to lift someone else up.

"Wherever we are in life, there are times when all of us have challenges and struggles. Although they are different for each, they are common to all," taught President Thomas S. Monson. "We were not placed on this earth to walk alone."[1]

You can tell the story of how you moved your mountain, and you can in turn help someone else to move theirs. We are

---

1. Thomas S. Monson, "We Never Walk Alone," *Ensign*, November 2013.

all in this human experience together. We are not alone; we ought to stop acting like we are.

Be open. Tell others about what you are struggling with. Tell them about your grief and your illness, your mistakes and your weaknesses. Ask for help. Let them serve you. Have the courage to be honest, authentic, and vulnerable. Own your problems so they don't own you.

And then listen! We are all in this club of loss together, you see. We have wasted so much of our lives trying to battle stoically in silence. My dad was so ashamed of his heart condition and diabetes that none of us knew how sick he was or how badly he was hurting. I've spent so many years trying to hide my OCD instead of facing the monster, head-on, that it has nearly taken my life and has already robbed me of a lifetime of opportunities and experiences.

We get stuck in the mindset that we cannot let others see how human, how vulnerable, how fallible we truly are. But we do not have to do this alone any longer. As we open up to each other, we open ourselves up to growth, connection, and change.

My dear friend, we are in this together now. We are on the same team. We are paddling the same waters in the sea of sorrow, even if your grief looks different from mine.

Here in the club of loss we face our hardest battles together.

Love,
Gabrielle

About the Author

GABRIELLE SHIOZAWA plans to spend her whole life bringing people together through stories. She is pursuing a bachelor's degree in journalism from Brigham Young University, where she endeavors to try new things and conquer her fears whenever possible. Gabrielle has been published in *YA Weekly*, *The Palouse Review*, the *Las Vegas Sun*, and *The Daily Universe*. Her favorite things in life include driving with the windows down, hugging people, and eating ice cream. This is her debut book. Follow her on Instagram @gabrielleshiozawa.